Fujifilm X-M5 User Handbook

A Comprehensive Guide with Step-by-Step Instructions and Professional Tips for Mastering Photography and Videography

Torren Mercy

CHAPTER ONE
OVERVIEW

The Fujifilm X-M5 overview

The Fujifilm X-M5 is a small, entry-level mirrorless camera made for vloggers and content producers as well as beginning photographers. You may utilize a variety of lenses from the company's large XF and XC lineups because it has the Fujifilm X mount. However, because it's smaller, it looks best with lighter, thinner lenses that don't overpower its little frame. This camera is a component of Fujifilm's efforts to create a user-friendly, portable device for producing high-quality photos and videos. The X-M5 doesn't cut corners on speed despite its little size. The fifth-generation X Processor 5 and a **potent 26.1MP** X-Trans CMOS 4 APS-C sensor are integrated. This camera improves processing speed and image quality while maintaining the same features as the Fujifilm X-S20. The X-M5 is smaller and lighter than the X-T30 II, but it features a more advanced processing engine. It is therefore a good option for those who desire flexibility without sacrificing strength. The X-M5 follows the X-S20's example by replacing the standard exposure features of cameras such as the Fujifilm X-T50 or X-T5 with a setting dial. Those who are new to photography will find it easy to move between shooting modes with this mode dial. Fujifilm's distinct film emulation modes can also be controlled separately with the X-M5's Film Simulation Mode slider. The X-T50 was the first to have this dial. This option allows users to instantly alter the color profiles of the camera, giving their images and videos a fresh appearance and feel. The absence of a viewfinder is a glaring shortcoming of the X-M5. For all framing and composition, the back LCD panel with variable-angle display must be utilized. Because of its tilt and rotate capabilities, this screen is ideal for vlogging, taking selfies, and taking unusual perspectives. This screen might not be to everyone's taste, though, as some individuals preferred to use a viewfinder for more precise composition. For photographers and filmmakers that appreciate versatility, ease of use, and the newest image technology, the X-M5 is designed to be simple and easy to operate.

To keep the Fujifilm X-M5 safe, the screen may be folded up against the camera's body.

Availability and Price of the Fujifilm X-M5

The price of the Fujifilm X-M5 body was £799 (US$799, €899, or $1,249) when it went on sale on November 14, 2024. It came with the XC 15-45mm F3.5-5.6 OIS PZ kit lens for £899 (US$899, €999, or $1,649). The XC 15-45mm F3.5-5.6 OIS PZ kit lens is only available in black; however Fujifilm produces the X-M5 in both silver and black.

Detailed specifications

- Announced: 14th October 2024
- Camera Type: Mirrorless
- Lens Mount: X-Mount
- Sensor: 26.1MP X-Trans 4 CMOS APS-C format sensor
- Processing Engine: X-Processor 5
- Sensitivity Range: ISO 125-12,800 (expandable to ISO 80-51,200)
- Viewfinder: None
- Screen: 3-inch Vari-angle LCD touchscreen with 1.04 million dots
- Autofocus System: Intelligent hybrid with up to 425 selectable AF points
- Subject Detection: Face/Eye AF, animals, birds, cars, motorcycles, bicycles, airplanes, trains, insects, and drones

- Continuous Shooting:
    - Mechanical Shutter: 8fps
    - Electronic Shutter: 30fps with 1.25x crop, 20fps full-sensor
- Max Video Resolution:
    - 6.2K (6240 x 4160) at 29.97/25/24/23.98fps
    - DCI 4K (4096 x 2160) at 59.95/50/29.97/25/24/23.98fps
    - 4K (3840 x 2160) at 59.95/50/29.97/25/24/23.98fps
- Stabilization: Digital Image Stabilization (DIS) Mode Boost for video only
- Storage: SD/SDHC/SDXC UHS-I
- Dimensions: 111.9 × 66.6 × 38.5mm
- Weight: 355g (including battery and card)

The Fujifilm X-M5 features a hinged 3-inch, 1.04-million-dot touch screen for taking and editing pictures or videos. You can tilt the screen up or down, flip it out to the side of the camera, or turn it around to face forward.

Important Features

Fujifilm's most recent news has focused on the new 40.2MP BSI CMOS 5 HR sensor, but the X-M5's 26.1MP X-Trans CMOS 4 sensor sets it apart. Although the X-M5 has the more potent X-Processor 5 engine, which is also found in the X-T50 and X-T5, which offers ring-improved performance, this sensor is also found in the X-S20, X-T4, and X-T30 II. You may use state-of-the-art capabilities like sophisticated autofocus and subject recognition systems for still and video images with this sensor and processing power. Animals, birds, automobiles, motorcycles, bicycles, trains, airplanes, insects, and drones are among the objects it can locate. The subject detection system of the X-M5 is incredibly adaptable. According to Fujifilm, this system, along with the most recent autofocus (AF) and subject recognition algorithms make the X-M5 superior to the X-S20. However, a firmware upgrade will be made for the X-S20 to match the X-M5's AF capabilities. The X-M5 can shoot continuously at high rates. The burst depth is 173 JPEGs or 25 raw RAW files, and the motorized shutter allows you to shoot at up to 8 frames per second. Using the automatic shutter increases the rate to 20 frames per second at full resolution, with a burst depth of 127 JPEGs or 23 raw RAW files. For even quicker speeds, the X-M5 can reach 30 frames per second when using a 1.25x crop mode. According to CIPA testing data, the NP-W126S battery can take up to 440 live pictures in economy mode, 330 live pictures in normal mode, and 300 live pictures in boost mode. The X-M5 supports 4K video at up to 60p and internal 6.2K 4:2:2 10-bit open gate recording at 30p. This enables the camera to use the full sensor area for video capture, giving it more flexibility when filming in varied aspect ratios. It is also possible to capture Full HD video at a stunning 240p, which results in stunning slow-motion footage. The most crucial facts are still made apparent and stand out thanks to this revised content arrangement. If you require any other adjustments, do let me know! For recording 4:2:2 10bit color video from an external source, there is also a Type D HDMI connector. Making movies is made easier with the X-M5's addition of the Vlog mode, which was initially introduced on the X-

S20. You may shoot video in portrait mode while holding the camera in landscape mode thanks to the new 9:16 Short Movie mode. This can be configured to record clips of 15, 30, or 60 seconds. Additionally, it features Background Defocus, Portrait Enhancer, and an improved microphone setup. New buttons in the Vlog mode Graphical User Interface (GUI) allow you to access both the old and new vlogging functionality. The Fujifilm X-M5 has three microphones. They can be used to record stereo sound to focus on sound from in front of or behind the camera or both. Also, these mics are reported to be better than earlier models, and the upgraded wind filter can cut out steady-state noise like an air conditioner's persistent hum. The X-M5 also contains a 3.5mm microphone jack and a 3.5mm headphone jack, which is wonderful news.

The X-M5 can capture 4K/30p footage for more than 60 minutes at 25 degrees Celsius. This time decreases to roughly 20 minutes at 40 degrees. On the other hand, the camera can be used with the Fujifilm Cooling Fan (FAN-001). When the temperature is 40 degrees, this extends the maximum recording duration to more than 60 minutes. Though it lacks optical in-camera stabilization, the X-M5 can use lens-based stabilization, and the lens recording ring allows for digital image stabilization. To further improve stabilization, there is also an IS Mode Boost setting. Since it must be cropped, of course, Digital Image Stabilization cannot be used in open gate mode. Depending on the frame rate, there is either a 1.32x or 1.44x crop when recording in 4K or Full HD. The rolling shutter can also be fixed by Digital Image Stabilization. PROVIA/Standard, Velvia/Vivid, ASTIA/Soft, Classic Chrome, REALA ACE, PRO Neg.Hi, PRO Neg.Std, Classic Neg., Nostalgic Neg., ETERNA/Cinema, ETERNA BLEACH BYPASS, ACROS, and ACROS + Ye Filter are among the 20 Fujifilm Film Simulation settings in the X-M5, which are popular with many users. Sepia, black and white, black and white plus a Ye filter, black and white plus a R filter, black and white plus a G filter. Both stills and video can be used with them. The X-M5's Multiple Exposure mode allows you to combine up to nine images in the camera using one of four mix modes: Additive, Average, Bright, and Dark. Fans of multiple exposure will love the four modes. Using its XApp app, Fujifilm has enabled the X-M5 to deliver files straight to smartphones over a USB-C cable. This is particularly useful for transmitting large files (more than 4GB) to iOS or Android tablets or phones in a timely manner. A new low-bitrate mode with 25 Mbps and 8 Mbps speeds has been introduced to facilitate the wireless sharing of smaller video files. The X-M5 can also be used as a camera when connected via USB-C.

The Fujifilm X-M5 sports a tiny joystick in place of a control pad on the back. This allows your thumb to rest on the camera's rear. Another good grip is the curvature on the right side of the camera. The mic port's lid is the black circle to the left and below the hotshoe.

The Build and Management

It's small and light—111.9 x 66.6 x 38.0 mm and 355g—and it's smaller and lighter than both the X-T30 II (118.4 x 82.8 x 46.8 mm and 378g) and the X-T50 (123.8 x 84 x4 8.8 mm and 438g). The X-M5 feels well-made and balanced, even though it's small and light. It has a thin but rather good front grip with a little thumb rest on the back. Both are approximately the perfect size and weight for the camera. The XC 15-45mm kit lens works excellent with the X-M5, but I don't like how the power zoom works when I use the lens ring. You have to zoom back in because it's too simple to miss the point you want to see. While capturing video and recording sound with the built-in microphone, the touchscreen zoom settings are superior. However, it's crucial to know that the zoom isn't silent, so you may pick up some sound if you adjust the focal length.

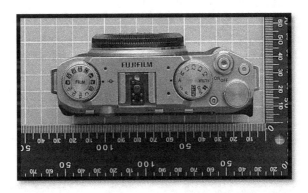

The Fujifilm X-M5 has two control knobs and dials for adjusting the exposure mode and the Film Simulation Mode. The first control wheel is on the extreme right side of the top plate, while the second one sticks out from the front of the camera, just below the power button and shutter button. The tiny thumb rest is seen in the lower right corner of this shot. I took pictures of dancing practice using the X-M5 and the XF50-140mm F2.8 R LM OIS WR, even though they don't work well together. I reflexively held the lens with my left hand while making settings changes with my right. For the tiny camera, the lens is rather large. Setting it up that way was workable, but not ideal. However, the smaller prime lenses made by Fujifilm would be a great fit for the camera. Although everyone has a different definition of beauty, I find the X-M5 to be a pretty small camera. The top plate features three knobs. The exposure mode dial is on the right, the Film Simulation mode dial is on the left, and a smaller control dial for setting changes is in the center. This final dial is compatible with a dial that protrudes above the grip from the front of the camera. This indicates that the exposure settings can be altered using the two buttons. Photojournalists accustomed to Fujifilm's touch controls will enjoy the upscale feel of these buttons.

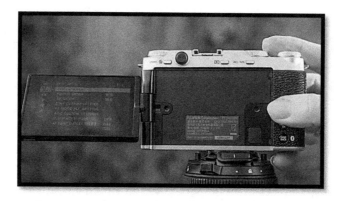

All of the Fujifilm X-M5's settings are conveniently located on the back. My thumb is on the key in this picture. The "Auto" setting on the exposure mode dial is useful for both novice and experienced photographers who are pressed for time. Upon selecting this option, the camera examines the scene and selects the optimal settings for the circumstances. Because of its small size, the X-M5 is unlikely to appeal to those with large hands. However, the buttons are easily accessible, and I had no trouble using them. However, when you run your thumb across the back of the camera, it's difficult to distinguish between the Menu/OK and Display/Back buttons. Although the screen is touch-sensitive and provides good control, a tiny joystick on the rear of the camera would be useful for navigating the menu, selecting settings, and adjusting the autofocus point. This is easy to locate and use, and it's in a good location. As I mentioned earlier, the X-M5 lacks a viewfinder. This is a major turnoff for a lot of shooters. It contributes to the camera's low weight, size, and cost. You must use the 3-inch, 1.4-million-dot image touch screen to frame and view images and videos.

The charging port, headphone jack, and small HDMI ports are located on the right side of the X-M5 (from the top down) when you hold it to use it. Moving all of the connection ports off of the left side of the camera was an innovative move by Fujifilm. In this manner, cables won't obstruct the flip-out screen's movement. A micro HDMI port, a headphone jack, and a charging port are located on the right side. The hotshoe has a microphone port underneath it. It goes without saying that using any of those ports will make it harder to hold the camera firmly. Generally speaking, though, you should only use the headphones when the camera is in a cage, on a tripod, or on a gimbal unless you really must. I discovered that a camera strap obscured my view of the screen when I joined it using the two strap lugs. The issue was resolved by attaching two Peak Design Anchor Loops to the right strap lug of the X-M5 and attaching the Peak Design Slide Lite to them. Because the X-M5's strap lugs are bar-shaped rather than tiny and require a split ring, this is simple to accomplish.

The Fujifilm X-M5's charge port, headphone jack, and mini HDMI port are all on the right side, which is not typical. The most popular Film Simulation modes, according to Fujifilm research, are ASTIA/SOFT, CLASSIC CHROME, REALA ACE, CLASSIC Neg., NOSTALGIC Neg., ACROS, PROVIA/STANDARD, and Velvia/VIVID. There are also eight preset Film Simulation modes that can be adjusted on the X-M5's Film Simulation dial. If your chosen Film Simulation mode isn't already selected, you can activate it using one of three customisable options (FS1, FS2, and FS3). The dial also features a "C" setting that enables you choose the Film Simulation Mode from the Main or Quick Menus. Within the menu, you can't pick Film Simulation mode if the dial is set to any other position than C. I shoot raw files, so I can adjust and tweak the Film Simulation Mode once I process the file. However, having the Film Simulation Mode slider there makes me more likely to switch between the settings when I'm shooting. My ability to visualize the final image or video is facilitated by this. This also increases the likelihood that my shots are ready to post immediately out of the camera, as I frequently take both raw and Jpeg photos simultaneously.

The X-M5's top plate has two dials: one for exposure mode on the right side and one for film simulation mode on the left.

About the Performance

Since the Fujifilm X-M5 shares the same sensor and processing engine as the X-S20, its speed and image quality are not particularly surprising. As a result, given its pixel count and sensor size, it can capture a large amount of data at low sensitivity (ISO) settings. Up to ISO 3200, there is also very little noise. JPEGs become slightly smoother over this threshold, but raw files exhibit higher brightness noise (speckling). In many cases, the image quality is good at ISO 6400 or even ISO 12,800. You can frequently leave the exposure compensation control alone because the X-M5's built-in Multi exposure-metering ring system performs admirably most of the time. However, while shooting outside in bright light, it can be challenging to determine the exposure because there is no viewfinder and you must use the screen. Although the histogram view can be useful, it is not as useful as seeing the image as you would like it to appear before taking the photo. The good dynamic range of the low-ISO raw files makes them useful. This indicates that you can achieve the desired look by adjusting them to a reasonable level, such as 2-3EV of brightness. People have always enjoyed the colors of Fujifilm's Film Simulation Modes. Provia/Standard is a good all-around option that creates colors that are similar to the scene and look natural. However, there are 19 additional options, so there is something for every setting, taste, and fashion sense. The earthy tones of Classic Chrome and the high contrast and low saturation of Eterna Bleach Bypass look great. Acros, on the other hand, delivers fantastic monochrome shots immediately out of the camera in live mode. Because of the poor light, the sensitivity level has to be pushed up to ISO 1000 or higher. However, the autofocus technology works swiftly and correctly. Additionally, subject recognition performs admirably, which is useful when you have to take immediate action. If you're recording video with the X-M5 in your hand, ensure that the Digital Image Stabilization (DIS) is turned on. I regret not checking it, even though I should have done so. The footage is slightly improved by the optical stabilization of the 15-45mm kit lens, but the DIS is absolutely necessary. The wind noise is evident in the video I recorded during a particularly windy moment, but it's not as bad as it has been with other cameras. When there was no wind, I would simultaneously wear a wind blocker and an external microphone.

A Q button on the top plate of the Fujifilm X-M5 allows you to access the Quick menu, which can be customized. You can easily locate it with your finger when you look at the back screen.

For whom is this camera intended?

Photographers, filmmakers, and content creators who desire a compact, lightweight camera without sacrificing quality are the target market for the Fujifilm X-M5. For those who want a gadget that can handle both photographs and movies, especially while they are on the road, its compact size and user-friendly design make it an excellent option. For those who are just starting out and wish to upgrade from a smartphone or point-and-shoot, the camera is a fantastic option. Although the design is user-friendly for novices, more seasoned users will appreciate its powerful features. The AI-enhanced autofocus system makes it easy to take sharp, focused photos even in low light, and the 26.1MP X-Trans CMOS 4 sensor produces excellent image quality. For vloggers who wish to produce high-quality videos, the X-M5 truly shines because of its 6.2K video recording. The camera's touchscreen, which can be used from various angles, makes self-recording simple and even more helpful for producers who work alone. With different directional audio settings to fit diverse recording conditions, the microphone system is another outstanding feature. Although the camera doesn't feature electronic viewfinder (EVF) or in-body image stabilization (IBIS), this won't deter many people from buying it, especially those who prefer to take images or videos in decent lighting using the Capture One Focus Ring. The X-M5 is a camera for those who want a powerful, feature-rich camera in a compact package, whether they're shooting for a business project, vlogging for YouTube, or simply capturing everyday moments with great image quality.

CHAPTER TWO

THE FUJIFILM X-M5: STARTING OFF

Understanding the Camera Parts

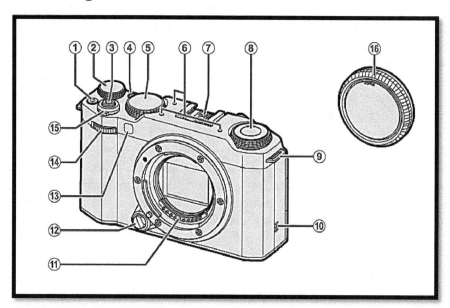

1. ⦿ (Movie recording) button
2. Rear command dial
3. Shutter button
4. [Q] Quick menu button
5. Mode dial
6. Microphone
7. Hot shoe
8. Film simulation dial
9. Strap eyelet
10. Speaker
11. Lens signal contacts
12. Lens release button
13. AF-assist illuminator
    ▪ Self-timer lamp
    ▪ Tally light
14. Front command dial
15. [ON/OFF] switch
16. Body cap

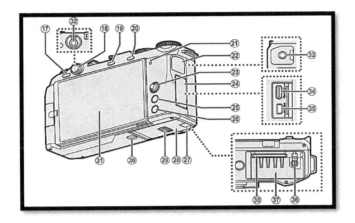

17. **[DRIVE]** button
    - 🗑 delete button
18. Microphone/remote release connector cover
19. ▶ (playback) button
20. [AEL] (exposure lock)/[AFL] (focus lock) button
21. Indicator lamp
    - Tally light
22. Headphone jack cover
23. Focus stick (focus lever)
24. Connector cover
25. [MENU/OK] button
26. [DISP] (display)/[BACK] button
    - 🅱 (bluetooth) button
27. Cable channel cover for DC coupler
28. Battery-chamber cover
29. Battery-chamber cover latch
30. Tripod mount
31. Vari-angle LCD monitor
    - Touch screen
32. Microphone/remote release connector (φ3.5mm)
33. Headphone jack (φ3.5 mm)
34. USB connector (Type-C)
35. HDMI Micro connector (Type D)
36. Battery latch
37. Battery chamber
38. Memory card slot

Keep in mind: In order to utilize an optional RR-100 remote release in **32**, change the three-pin, φ2.5 mm connector to a three-pin, φ3.5 mm connector using a third-party adapter.

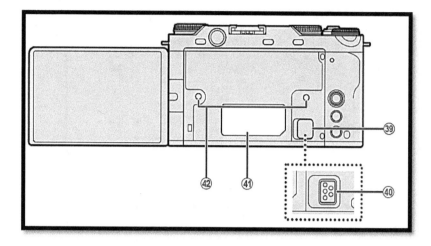

39. Cooling fan connector cover
40. Cooling fan connector
41. Serial number plate
42. Hole to screw cooling fan

Displays for Cameras

The signs that could appear while shooting are listed in this section.

The following are the displays presented with all indicators lit for illustrative purposes:

The LCD Monitor

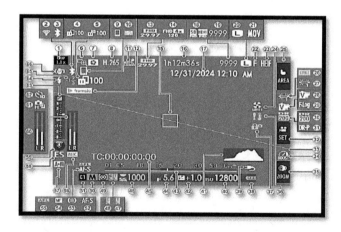

1. Crop factor
2. Wireless connection
3. Bluetooth ON/OFF

4. Image transfer status
5. Frame.io upload progress
6. Focus check
7. Depth-of-field preview
8. Movie compression
9. Bluetooth host
10. AirGlu BT connection
11. Location data download status
12. Frame.io connection status
13. Movie mode
14. High-speed recording indicator
15. Focus frame
16. Recording time available/elapsed recording time
17. Date and time
18. Destination for movie recording
19. Number of available frames[1]
20. Image size
21. File format
22. Image quality
23. HEIF format
24. Cooling fan settings
25. Touch screen mode[3]
26. AWB lock
27. White balance
28. Film simulation
29. F-Log/HLG recording
30. Dynamic range
31. D-range priority
32. Movie optimized control[3]
33. Virtual horizon
34. Boost mode
35. Touch zoom[3]
36. Temperature warning
37. Control lock[4]
38. Battery level
39. Power supply
40. Sensitivity
41. Histogram
42. Exposure compensation
43. Distance indicator[2]
44. Aperture
45. Time code
46. Shutter speed

47. TTL lock
48. AE lock
49. Metering
50. Shooting mode
51. Custom modes
52. Focus mode[2]
53. Focus indicator[2]
54. Manual focus indicator[2]
55. AF lock
56. Microphone input channel
57. AF+MF indicator[2]
58. Shutter type
59. Microphone direction
60. Recording level[2]
61. Continuous mode
62. Self-timer indicator
63. Exposure indicator
64. Flash (TTL) mode
65. Flash compensation
66. IS mode[2]

Design note

The LCD monitor

- Displays "9999" if there is room for more than 9999 frames.
- Not shown when 🖪 [SCREEN SET-UP] > [LARGE INDICATORS MODE(LCD)] is set to [ON].
- Touch controls are also available for navigating camera features.
- Shown when the [MENU/OK] button is pressed and held to lock the controls. To exit control lock, press and hold the [MENU/OK] button one more.

Modifying the Brightness of the Display

When worn outdoors, light sources like sunlight may make the display difficult to see. In the 🖪 [SCREEN SET-UP] menu, use [LCD BRIGHTNESS] and [LCD COLOR] to adjust the LCD monitor's brightness and saturation.

Rotating the Display

The LCD monitor's indicators automatically rotate to align with the camera orientation when [ON] is chosen for 🖪 [SCREEN SET-UP] > [AUTOROTATE DISPLAYS].

The Button for [DISP/BACK]

The LCD monitor's indication display is managed via the [DISP/BACK] button.

Info display (still photography only)

Standard indicators

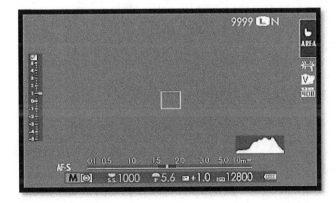

No indicators

Personalizing Indicators for Displays

To select the objects displayed in the typical indicator display:

❖ [DISP. CUSTOM SETTING] is selected.

    A. From the setup menu, choose 🎬 [SCREEN SET-UP] > [DISP. CUSTOM SETTING].

❖ Select items

    ▪ To choose or deselect items, highlight them and click [MENU/OK].
- [FRAMING GUIDELINE]
- [FOCUS FRAME]
- [FOCUS INDICATOR]
- [AF DISTANCE INDICATOR]
- [MF DISTANCE INDICATOR]
- [HISTOGRAM]
- [LIVE VIEW HIGHLIGHT ALERT]
- [SHOOTING MODE]
- [APERTURE/S-SPEED/ISO]
- [INFORMATION BACKGROUND]
- [Expo. Comp. (Digit)]
- [Expo. Comp. (Scale)]
- [FOCUS MODE]
- [PHOTOMETRY]
- [SHUTTER TYPE]
- [FLASH]
- [CONTINUOUS MODE]
- [DUAL IS MODE]
- [TOUCH SCREEN MODE]
- **Vlog** [PLAY BACK BUTTON]
- **Vlog** [REC BUTTON]
- **Vlog** [MENU BUTTON]
- [WHITE BALANCE]
- [FILM SIMULATION]

- o [DYNAMIC RANGE]
- o [BOOST MODE]
- o [COOLING FAN SETTING]
- o [FRAMES REMAINING]
- o [IMAGE SIZE/QUALITY]
- o [MOVIE MODE & REC. TIME]
- o [COMMUNICATION STATUS]
- o [MIC LEVEL]
- o [MICROPHONE DIRECTION SETTING]
- o [GUIDANCE MESSAGE]
- o [NO STORAGE MEDIA WARNING]
- o [DATE/TIME]
- o [BATTERY LEVEL]
- o [FRAMING OUTLINE]
- ❖ In order to save modifications, press [DISP/BACK].

Framing Outline

To make the frame's edges more visible against dark backgrounds, enable [FRAMING OUTLINE].

Histograms

Histograms display the image's tone distribution. The horizontal axis displays brightness, while the vertical axis displays the number of pixels.

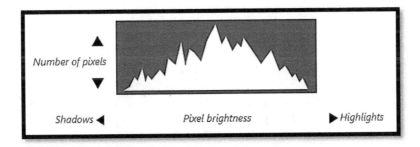

- ❖ **Optimal exposure:** The tone range is covered by pixels arranged in an even curve.

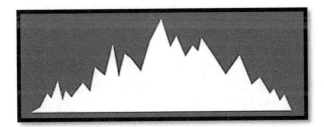

❖ **Overexposed:** The graph's right side has a concentration of pixels.

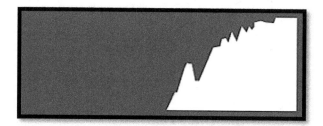

❖ **Underexposed:** Pixels are concentrated on the left side of the graph.

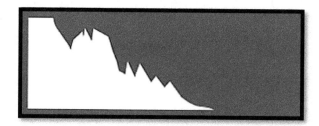

Press the function button to which [HISTOGRAM] is assigned to view individual RGB histograms and a display that overlays the view through the lens with parts of the picture that will be overexposed at current settings.

1. Blinking in overexposed areas
2. RGB histograms

The Horizon Virtual

Verify the camera's levelness. ▣ [SCREEN SET-UP] > [ELECTRONIC LEVEL SETTING] can be used to select the type of display. When putting the camera on a tripod or similar device, use the virtual horizon to level the camera.

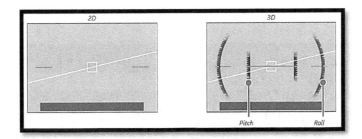

- ❖ **[OFF]:** There is no virtual horizon visible.
- ❖ **[2D]:** The degree of left or right camera tilt is shown by a white line. When the camera is level, the line turns green. If the camera is angled forward or backward, the line can disappear.
- ❖ **[3D]:** The screen indicates if the camera is angled forward or backward and left or right.

Note: One way to switch between the 2D and 3D displays is to assign [ELECTRONIC LEVEL SWITCH] to a function button.

About the Menus

Press [MENU/OK] to bring up the menus.

Utilizing Menus

Various menus appear when taking still photography, recording movies, and playback.
- ❖ Still photography

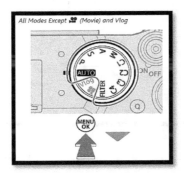

- While taking still photography, click [MENU/OK] to see the photo menus.

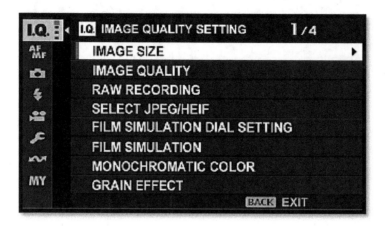

- Picture menus will appear in modes [C1] through [C4] if ▣ [STILL] is selected for the selected bank using either ▣ [MOVIE SETTING] > ▣▣ [CUSTOM MODE SETTING] in the movie menus or ▣ [IMAGE QUALITY SETTING] > ▣▣ [CUSTOM MODE SETTING] in the picture menus.

❖ **Movies Recording**

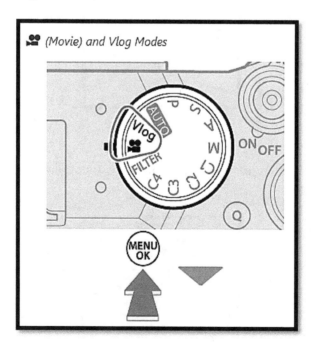

- The movie menus are displayed when you click [MENU/OK] in movie mode.

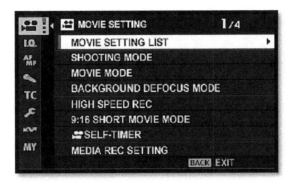

- Photo menus will appear in modes [C1] through [C4] if [MOVIE] is selected for the selected bank using either [MOVIE SETTING] > [CUSTOM MODE SETTING] in the movie menus or [IMAGE QUALITY SETTING] > [CUSTOM MODE SETTING] in the photo menus.

❖ **Playback**

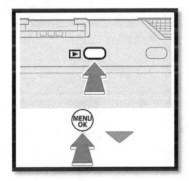

- The playback menu is displayed when you press [MENU/OK] while the playback is running.

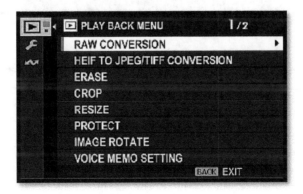

Choosing a Menu Tab

To use the menus:

❖ The options will appear when you press [MENU/OK].

❖ To highlight the current menu tab, press the left focus stick (focus lever).

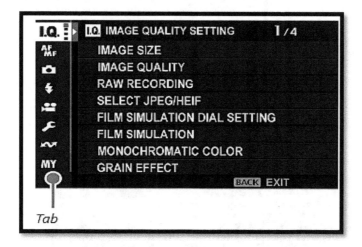

❖ To draw attention to the tab that contains the required item, move the focus stick up or down.

❖ To position the cursor in the menu, use the right focus stick button.

Note: To navigate through menus or choose menu tabs, use the front command dial; to highlight menu items, use the rear command dial.

Mode of Touch Screen

Additionally, the LCD monitor can be used as a touch screen.

Touch Controls for Shooting

Choose [ON] for 🔧 [BUTTON/DIAL SETTING] > [TOUCH SCREEN SETTING] > 📷 [TOUCH SCREEN SETTING] to activate touch controls.

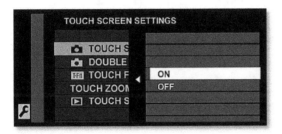

LCD Display

By tapping the touch screen mode indicator on the screen, you can choose the operation that was carried out. **The following tasks can be performed with touch controls:**

	Mode	Description
👆SHOT	**[TOUCH SHOOTING]**	Tap your subject in the display to focus and release the shutter. In burst mode, pictures will be taken while you keep your finger on the display.
👆AF	**[AF]**	• If **[SINGLE AF]** is selected for focus mode, the camera will focus when you tap your subject in the display. Focus locks at the current distance until you tap the **[AF OFF]** icon.
⬆⬇		• If **[CONTINUOUS AF]** is selected for focus mode, the camera will initiate focus when you tap your subject in the display. The camera will continue to adjust focus for changes in the distance to the subject until you tap the **[AF OFF]** icon.
👆AF OFF	**[AF OFF]**	• When **[MANUAL FOCUS]** is selected for focus mode, you can tap the display to focus on the selected subject using autofocus.
👆AREA	**[AREA]**	Tap to select a point for focus or zoom. The focus frame will move to the selected point.
👆OFF	**[OFF]**	Touch screen mode off.

Design note:

- ❖ Depending on the AF mode, the touch screen behaves differently.
- ❖ During focus zoom, various touch controls are utilized
- ❖ Choose [OFF] for 🅕 [BUTTON/DIAL SETTING] > [TOUCH SCREEN SETTING] > 📷 [TOUCH SCREEN SETTING] to turn off touch controls and conceal the touch screen mode indicator.
- ❖ You can zoom in by touching the monitor twice when [ON] is set for 🅕 [BUTTON/DIAL SETTING] > [TOUCH SCREEN SETTING] > 📷 [DOUBLE TAP SETTING].
- ❖ 🔲 [AF/MF SETTING] > [TOUCH SCREEN MODE] allows you to change the touch control settings.

[OPTIMIZED MOVIE CONTROL] 🔘🔧

For 🎬 [MOVIE SETTING] > [MOVIE OPTIMIZED CONTROL], choose [ON] 🔘🔧 or pressing the shooting display's movie-optimized mode button enhances the touch controls and command dials for filming. This can be used to stop movie footage from recording camera sounds.

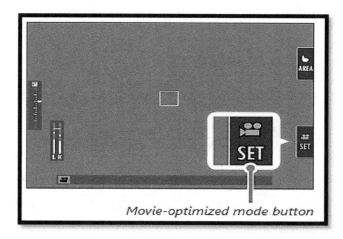

Movie-optimized mode button

- ❖ [SHUTTER SPEED]
- ❖ [APERTURE]
- ❖ [EXPOSURE COMPENSATION]
- ❖ 🎬 [ISO]
- ❖ [INTERNAL MIC LEVEL ADJUSTMENT]/
- ❖ [EXTERNAL MIC LEVEL ADJUSTMENT]
- ❖ [WIND FILTER]

- ❖ [STEADY-STATE NOISE REDUCTION]
- ❖ [LOW CUT FILTER]
- ❖ [HEADPHONES VOLUME]
- ❖ 🎥 [FILM SIMULATION]
- ❖ 🎥 [WHITE BALANCE]
- ❖ 🎥 [IS MODE]
- ❖ 🎥 [IS MODE BOOST]
- ❖ 🎥 [FOCUS MODE]

Design note:
- ❖ The aperture ring is turned off when movie-optimized settings are enabled.
- ❖ The movie-optimized mode button can be used to switch shooting settings or turn off movie-optimized control while it is active.
- ❖ Only when an external microphone is connected may [EXTERNAL MIC LEVEL ADJUSTMENT] be adjusted.

The Touch Function

Similar to function buttons, the following flick motions can be assigned functions.

- • Flick up: **[T-Fn1]**
- • Flick left: **[T-Fn2]**
- • Flick right: **[T-Fn3]**
- • Flick down: **[T-Fn4]**

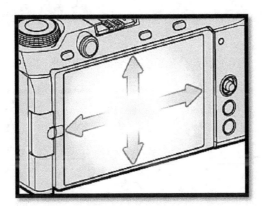

Design note:
- ❖ Touch-function flick motions can sometimes display a menu; tap to choose the option you want.

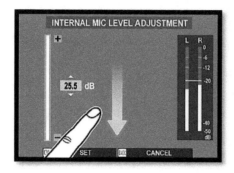

❖ By default, touch-function gestures are not enabled. Choose [ON] for [BUTTON/DIAL SETTING] > [TOUCH SCREEN SETTING] > [TOUCH FUNCTION] to activate touch-function gestures.

About Touch Zoom

You can touch the screen to zoom in and out if the lens has touch zoom. To activate touch zoom, tap the button on the screen.

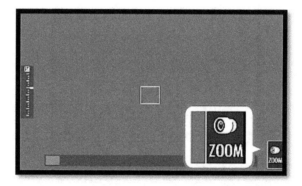

The buttons on the screen are used to control touch zoom.

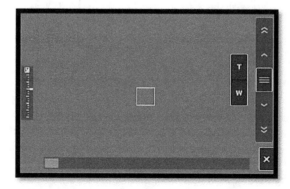

Button		Description
ZOOM	Touch zoom	Enable touch zoom.
T	Zoom in	Zoom in or out. Touch and hold to zoom in or out at a constant speed.
W	Zoom out	
(rocker switch icon)	Rocker switch	The camera zooms in or out at a speed corresponding to the position of the rocker switch.
X	Disable	Disable touch zoom.

Note: ⚙ [BUTTON/DIAL SETTING] > can be used to choose how quickly the camera zooms in and out in response to the [T] and [W] buttons. [CONSTANT SPEED ZOOM (Fn)] > [LENS ZOOM/FOCUS SETTING].

Touch Controls for Playback

Touch controls can be utilized for the following playback actions when [ON] is chosen for ⚙ [BUTTON/DIAL SETTING] > [TOUCH SCREEN SETTING] > ▶ [TOUCH SCREEN SETTING]:

❖ **Make a swipe:** To see more photographs, move your fingers around the screen.

❖ **Pinch-out:** To zoom in, place two fingers on the screen and spread them apart.

27

❖ **Pinch-in:** To zoom out, place two fingers on the screen and slide them together.

Note: Images can be enlarged to the farthest extent possible, but not beyond that.
   ❖ **Tap twice:** To enlarge the focus point, tap the screen twice.

Drag: Zoom in on various parts of the image as its playing.

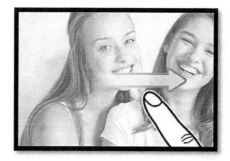

CHATER THREE
PRELIMINARY CAMERA CONFIGURATION

Putting on the Strap

How to put on the strap

As indicated below, fasten the strap to the two strap eyelets.

Cautions:
- ❖ Make sure the strap is securely fastened to prevent dropping the camera.
- ❖ The strap buckles should not be fastened to the strap eyelets. The strap eyelets could break or deform if this precaution is not followed.

Lens Attachment

- ❖ The camera is compatible with FUJIFILM X-mount lenses.
- ❖ Take off the lens's rear cap and the camera's body cap. With the markers on the lens and camera in alignment (1), place the lens on the mount. Then, slowly rotate the lens in the direction of the arrow until it snaps into place (2).

Cautions:
- ❖ Make sure that no dust or other foreign objects get inside the camera when you are adding lenses.
- ❖ Take cautious not to touch the internal components of the camera.
- ❖ Make sure the lens clicks firmly into position by rotating it.

❖ When connecting the lens, avoid pressing the lens release button.

How to remove the lenses

Turn off the camera, push the lens release button (1), and then slowly rotate the lens as shown (2) to remove it.

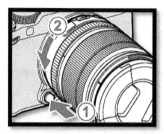

Caution: When the lens is not attached, replace the lens covers and camera body cap to avoid dust building up on the lens or within the camera.

Lenses & Additional Add-on Accessories

The camera is compatible with FUJIFILM X-mount lenses and accessories.
Cautions: When putting on or taking off (exchanging) lenses, take the following safety measures.

❖ Verify that there is no dust or other debris on the lenses.
❖ Avoid changing your lenses in bright light or in direct sunlight. The camera may malfunction if light is directed into its interior.
❖ Before switching lenses, fasten the lens caps.
❖ Holding movable components of the camera, such the aperture ring, while rotating the lens is not advised.
❖ For instructions on how to use the lens, consult the handbook that came with it.

Putting a memory card and battery in

As explained below, insert the memory card and batteries.
   A. **Lift the cover of the battery chamber:** The battery-chamber cover can be opened by sliding the latch as indicated.

Cautions:

- When the camera is turned on, avoid opening the battery-chamber cover. Image files or memory cards could be harmed if this precaution is not followed.
- When handling the battery-chamber cover, don't use too much force.

B. As indicated, insert the battery.

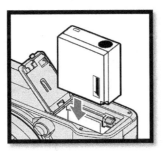

Cautions:

- Place the battery in the indicated position. Never try to put the battery in backwards or upside down, or use force.
- Verify that the battery is fastened firmly.

C. Put the memory card in

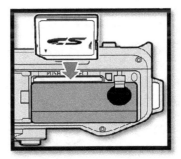

D. Slide the battery-chamber latch shut after closing the battery-chamber cover.

Caution: Verify that the battery is oriented correctly if the lid does not close. Don't try to push the cover closed.

Taking the Battery Out

Press the battery clasp to the side, slide the battery out of the camera, turn off the camera, and open the battery-chamber cover.

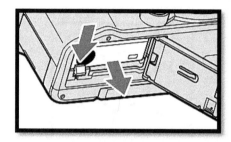

Note: When the battery is utilized in hot conditions, it could get heated. Be careful when taking the battery out.

Taking the Memory Card Out

After turning off the camera, open the cover of the battery compartment. Insert the memory card, slowly release it, and then manually remove it.

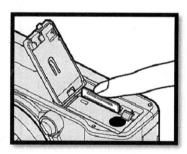

Cautions:
- Press the card's center.
- The card may slip out of the slot if you abruptly remove your finger from it. Slowly take your finger off.
- The memory card could feel heated to the touch if the camera shows an 🌡 icon. Do not remove the card until it has cooled.

Memory Cards That Are Compatible

❖ Memory cards that support SD, SDHC, and SDXC can be utilized with the camera.
❖ UHS-I memory cards are compatible with the camera.

❖ Depending on the parameters chosen, different memory card kinds are appropriate for recording movies.
❖ The Fujifilm website lists the memory cards that are compatible.

Precautions:
❖ When the memory card is being formatted or data is being recorded to or erased from the card, do not turn off the camera or take the card out. The card could be harmed if this precaution is not followed.
❖ Memory cards can be locked, which prevents you from recording or deleting photographs or formatting the card. Slide the write-protect switch to the unlocked position before putting in a memory card.

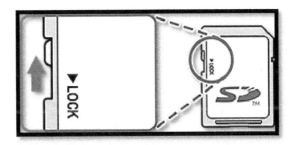

❖ Keep memory cards out of children's reach because they are small and easily swallowed. In the event that a child swallows a memory card, get medical help right away.
❖ Memory cards may not eject normally when miniSD or microSD adapters larger or smaller than the card are used; if this is the case; take the camera to an authorized service agent. Don't take the card away with force.
❖ Labels and other items should not be attached to memory cards. Camera malfunctions can be caused by peeling labels.
❖ Some memory card types have the potential to interrupt movie recording.
❖ When a photo is captured for the first time, the camera formats a memory card, creating a folder in which the pictures are stored. This folder should not be changed or removed, nor should picture files be edited, removed, or renamed via a computer or other device. Always erase photos with the camera; copy files to a computer before editing or renaming them, then modify or rename the copies, not the originals. Playback issues may arise if the camera's files are renamed.

About Battery Charging

When the battery is shipped, it is not charged. Before using the battery, charge it.
Note: The camera comes with a rechargeable battery (NP-W126S).
❖ You may use USB to charge the camera. Computers that have a USB interface and an operating system certified by the manufacturer can be charged over USB.

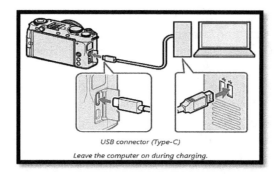

USB connector (Type-C)
Leave the computer on during charging.

- When the camera is turned on, the battery won't charge.
- Use a third-party USB cable to connect.
- Instead of using a USB hub or keyboard, connect the camera straight to the computer.
- If the computer goes into sleep mode, charging will halt. Turn on the computer and unplug and re-plug the USB cable to start charging again.
- Depending on the computer's model, settings, and present condition, charging might not be supported.
- With a charging input of 5 V/500 mA, the battery takes roughly 300 minutes to charge.
- ❖ Use a BC-W126S battery charger (separately available) to charge the battery from a domestic AC power outlet.

Charging Status

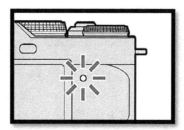

The battery charge state is displayed via the indicator bulb as follows:

Indicator lamp	Battery status
On	Battery charging
Off	Charging complete
Blinks	Charging error

- Labels and other items should not be attached to the battery. The camera's battery may not be able to be removed if this precaution is not followed.
- The battery terminals should not be shorted. The battery can get too hot.
- Go over the warnings in "For Your Safety."
- Only use authentic Fujifilm rechargeable batteries that are made specifically for this camera. If this precaution is not followed, the product may malfunction.
- Never try to fracture or peel the battery's exterior case, nor take off the labels.
- When not in use, the battery progressively loses its charge. One or two days prior to use, charge the battery.
- The battery has reached the end of its charging life and needs to be replaced if it can no longer hold a charge.
- Using a fresh, dry towel, wipe the battery terminals clean. If this precaution is not followed, the battery may not be able to charge.
- Keep in mind that both high and low temperatures lengthen charging times.
- The battery drain is increased when you choose [ON] for [Bluetooth/SMARTPHONE SETTING] > [Bluetooth ON/OFF] in the network/USB settings menu.

Note:
- ❖ The camera will stop charging and be powered by the USB connection if it is turned on while charging. There will be a progressive decrease in battery level.
- ❖ When the camera is powered by USB, a "power supply" icon will appear.

Activating and Deactivating the Camera

- ❖ **The camera can be turned on and off using the [ON/OFF] switch:** The camera can be turned on or off by sliding the switch to [ON] or [OFF].

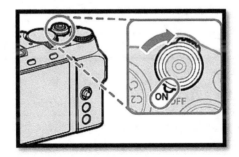

Caution: Images may be impacted by fingerprints and other lens blemishes. Make sure the lens is clean.

❖ Playback begins when the  button is pressed during shooting.

❖ In order to go back to shooting mode, press the shutter button halfway.

❖ If no actions are taken for the duration chosen for 🔧 [POWER MANAGEMENT] > [AUTO POWER OFF], the camera will shut off on its own. After the camera has automatically switched off, you can either push the shutter button halfway or flip the [ON/OFF] switch from [ON] to [OFF] and back to [ON] to turn it back on.

Verifying the Battery Level

Verify the battery level on the screen after turning on the camera.
This is how the battery level is displayed:

Indicator	Description
⬛🔋	Battery partially discharged.
🔋	Battery about 80% full.
🔋	Battery about 60% full.
🔋	Battery about 40% full.
🔋	Battery about 20% full.
🔋 (red)	Low battery. Charge as soon as possible.
🔋 (blinks red)	Battery exhausted. Turn camera off and recharge battery.

The Basic Configuration

You have the option to select a language and adjust the camera clock when you initially switch it on.

To switch on the camera for the first time, follow the instructions below.

❖ **Activate the camera:** A dialog box for choosing a language will appear.

❖ **Select a language:** Select a language to highlight, and then click [MENU/OK].

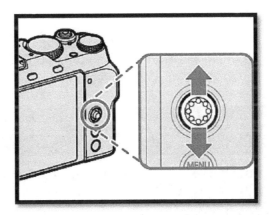

❖ **Select a time zone:** Select a time zone when requested, use the focus stick (focus lever) to turn on or off daylight savings time, then select [SET] and hit [MENU/OK].

- Press [DISP/BACK] to bypass this stage.
❖ **Set your clock:** In order to move on to the next step, press [MENU/OK].

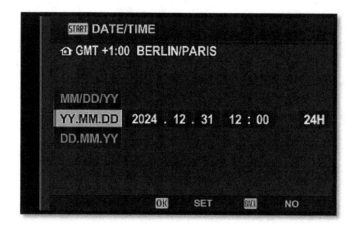

❖ **Check out the details on the mobile app.**
  - A QR code will appear on the camera, which you can scan with your phone to access a website where you may download the app.
  - In order to move on to the next step, press [MENU/OK].

Note: Utilize the smartphone app to remotely control the camera or download images from it.

❖ **A [AUTO POWER OFF TEMP] should be selected.**
  - The temperature at which the camera will automatically switch off depends on the setting that is chosen.
  - To exit to the shooting display, press [MENU/OK].

❖ **The memory card should be formatted.**
  ▪ Make careful to reformat all memory cards after using them in a computer or other device, and format them before using them for the first time.
  ▪ The camera clock will be reset and the language-selection dialog will appear when the camera is turned on if the battery is unplugged for a long time.

Fundamental Configuration and Setup

Turning on and establishing the initial configuration

Press the power button on the top of the camera after inserting your card and batteries. You will be asked to enter the time and date when you turn on the camera for the first time. This data can be manually entered or, if required, synchronized with the camera's internal clock.

Selecting the Language and Area

Turn on the Power Ring and choose your preferred language and locale. This is particularly important when changing the camera's time zone because it will help time-stamped photos and videos sync. Update this setting if you plan to travel or use the camera abroad to prevent confusion caused by regional differences in date formatting.

Establishing the Time and Date

You can choose the time and date on the X-M5, which is useful for arranging your photos and videos. By choosing "Time & Date" from the menu, you can modify this at any time.

Selecting Image Quality Settings

Once your basic setup is complete, navigate to the "Image Quality" settings in the menu. You can choose between RAW, JPEG, or both with the X-M5. While JPEG is appropriate for quick distribution without requiring a lot of manipulation, RAW provides the highest image quality and more post-processing options. Many users begin by shooting in JPEG for ease, however RAW is encouraged if you want the finest image quality for future editing.

Choosing Film Simulations

The unique Film Simulation modes on Fujifilm cameras are well-known for simulating the appearance of film. These may be accessible via the customized dial on top of the camera. While Acros and Classic Chrome offer a more muted vintage look, others like Velvia, Astia, and Provia offer vibrant color representations. Feel free to experiment and modify them to suit your creative vision. The default Provia setting is usually the easiest for beginners to use. Setting Auto Focus Subject Focus (AF) is one of the most important settings on the X-M5 because of its AI-driven autofocus technology, which can quickly adapt to various subjects. The menu allows you to choose between Manual Focus, Continuous AF, and Single AF. Continuous AF is recommended for moving subjects or video to ensure the subject stays in focus, while single AF is appropriate for general photography. In order to increase focus accuracy, you can also adjust the AF area. While "Zone" or "Spot" AF offers more precise control, especially when focusing on small or far-off objects, "Wide/Tracking" mode is best for general use.

The Setup Menus

User Setting

Change the camera's basic settings. Select MENU/OK, SET UP, and then USER SETTING to view the camera's default settings.

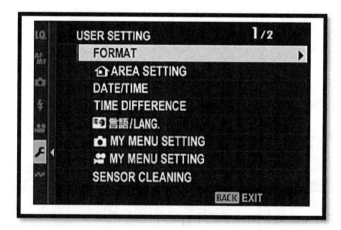

A. FORMAT
B. AREA SETTING

C. DATE/TIME
D. TIME DIFFERENCE
E. MY MENU SETTING
F. SENSOR CLEANING
G. SOUND & FLASH
H. FIRMWARE UPDATE
I. RESET
J. REGULATORY

The Format

Select this option, then, if there is a card slot, click OK to format a memory card. Pressing and holding the TRASH button takes about two and a half to three seconds. Then press and hold the button with the back command dial. This will take you straight to the Format option (or the Card Slot Selection option, if applicable). Every time you insert a new memory card into your camera, I always advise cleaning it. This reduces the likelihood of making a mistake and cleans the card. Since you have to start over each time, it's a terrific habit to develop.

To format a memory card, follow these steps:
  ❖ Select the FORMAT option under the SET UP menu. A confirmation dial box will appear.
  ❖ Select OK after selecting MENU/OK to format the card.

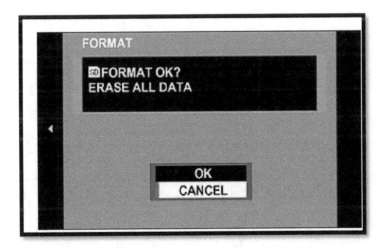

Press CANCEL or DISP/BACK to exit the program without erasing the memory card.
  ❖ All data, including password-protected images, will be erased from the memory card. A computer or other device should be used to store copies of crucial documents.
  ❖ When formatting, keep the cover above the battery compartment closed.
The format menu can also be seen by simultaneously pressing and holding the DRIVE button and the center of the back command dial. What would happen if you filled a card

only halfway with 200 frames? To get rid of the old photos, you could either do the "delete image" dance a hundred times or pull out the card and waste half the room. Or, worse (as it happened to me), you capture ten lovely pictures with a fully loaded card and then realize you forgot to format it. There may not be enough room for you. What if, at that moment, that was the only card you were carrying? Isn't it clear where this is headed? This is not the boat you want to be on. Believe me. Organize your cards.

Setting of the Area

To reflect your current time zone, change the settings.

Setting of the Zone

From the map, select your time zone.

Daylight Saving Time

Activate or deactivate daylight saving time.

Time and Date

- ❖ Go to the Adjust UP menu and choose USER SETTING > DATE/TIME to change the camera's clock.
- ❖ Slide the focus stick (lever) to the left or right to choose the day, hour, minute, month, or year. Move the focus stick up or down to make adjustments. Highlight the date style and move the focus stick to rearrange the day, month, and year on the screen.
- ❖ Click MENU/OK to set the time.

Difference in Time

You can switch the camera's time zone from HOME to LOCAL using this option. You can specify how much time has elapsed between your HOME and LOCAL timings when you select that menu item. This is an excellent idea when you move because it updates your record times to reflect the new time. It will appear to have been taken at 6:00 a.m. if you take a picture at noon while you are six time zones ahead. This option will spare you the hassle; however you can change the time the shot was taken using programs like Lightroom and shot Mechanic. Selecting LOCAL will cause the time and date to appear briefly in yellow each time the camera is turned on. This feature is fantastic. You can see what time zone you are in with that helpful notice. When you arrive home, it will be easier for you to remember to change it back.

My Menu Setting

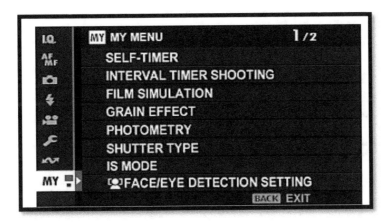

A great menu improvement is the new MY MENU. Regularly used settings can be saved in 16 distinct places. Anything you add to your MY MENU will be the first item shown when you turn on the camera and hit the MENU/OK button. This is essentially the fastest method for accessing the camera's settings and features. It only takes one button press to acquire the setting you want if you place it close to the top. This is quicker than any Fn button or the Q menu. Then scroll down to see the following items. Note: The next time you visit your MY MENU, it will take you to the last setting you updated if you have been using or exploring it. It will continue to operate in this manner until you switch the camera off and back on. You can add, remove, and rearrange items in the USER SETTING section of the MY MENU page. All you have to do is select an item from the camera menu by pressing ADD ITEMS. (Things that are already in your MY MENU have a checkbox next to them, and things that are available are indicated in blue.)

Press RANK items, select an item from MY MENU, and then OK, the "right" button, or the appropriate key to rearrange the items. Now that it's highlighted in yellow, you can use the joysticks up and down buttons to move it to a different location. When you're done, either press OK or return to the left using the buttons or keys. Simply select an item, click REMOVE ITEMS, and then click OK to remove it.

Cleaning Sensors

You can specify here how you would like the sensors cleaned. Depending on how the options in this menu are set up, you can either switch the camera on or off, and the operation can start right away when you push the OK button. It consists of electromagnetic waves, vibrations, subatomic energy, and small gnomes with brushes.

Option	Description
[OK]	Clean the sensor immediately.
[WHEN SWITCHED ON]	Sensor cleaning will be performed when the camera is turned on.
[WHEN SWITCHED OFF]	Sensor cleaning will be performed when the camera turns off (sensor cleaning is not however performed if the camera turns off in playback mode).

Flash and Sound

Simply turn off the camera lights and sounds if they annoy you. This will switch off the self-timer lighting, speaker, flashlight, and floodlight.

Update for Firmware

Use software stored on a memory card to modify the camera, lenses, and other components.

About Reset

This restores the default values for every parameter in the SHOOTING and SET UP menus. The custom settings banks and custom white balance that you created via the EDIT/SAVE CUSTOM SETTING, WIRELESS SETTINGS, DATE/TIME, and TIME DIFFERENCE choices won't be impacted.
   ❖ **Select the option you want to use, and then click MENU/OK.**
      ▪ MENU RESET STILL OCCURS. Return all picture menu settings to their original defaults, with the exception of custom white balance and custom settings banks created with xEDIT/SAVE CUSTOM SETTING.
      ▪ RESET MOVIE MENU Return all movie menu settings to their original settings, with the exception of custom white balance and custom settings banks created with FEDIT/SAVE CUSTOM SETTING.

- Configuration Reset: Return all setup menu settings to their initial values, with the exception of DATE/TIME, bAREA SETTING, TIME DIFFERENCE, and COPYRIGHT INFO.
- INITIZE: Return all settings to their initial settings, with the exception of custom white balance.

❖ Select OK from the confirmation window that appears, and then click MENU/OK.

Regulatory

Select REGULATORY from the SETTINGS menu to view electronic copies of the product model number and other certificates.

CHAPTER FOUR
FUNDAMENTAL PLAYBACK AND PHOTOGRAPHY

Taking your Pictures

Basic photography is explained in this section.

A. To see the 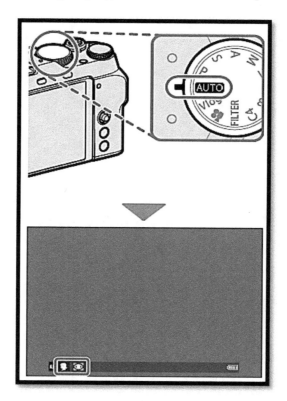 AUTO shooting display, turn the mode dial to [AUTO].

The type of scene and focus target detected will be shown by the camera.

Note: The camera constantly shifts focus and looks for eyes when in AUTO ([AUTO]) mode, which drains the battery more quickly. You can also hear the camera concentrating.

B. **Get the camera ready**
  - Using both hands to hold the camera steadily will help you avoid blurry photos.
  - Keep your fingers and other things away from the lens and AF-assist illuminator to avoid out-of-focus or underexposed photos.

C. **Set the photo in a frame.**
- **Zoom rings on lenses:** To frame the image on the screen, use the zoom ring. To zoom in or out, turn the ring to the left or right.

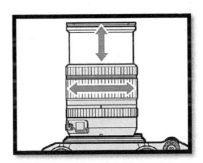

D. **Focus:** To focus, press the shutter button halfway.

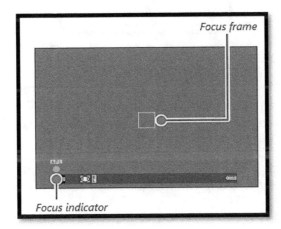

Focus frame

Focus indicator

❖ The focus frame and focus indicator will illuminate green if the camera can focus.

❖ The focus indication will blink white, the focus frame will become red, and s will appear if the camera cannot focus.
❖ The AF-assist illumination may illuminate to help with the focus operation if the subject is dimly lit.
❖ Halfway press of the shutter button will lock focus and exposure. When the button is held in this position, focus and exposure are locked (AF/AE lock).
❖ The macro and regular focus ranges of the lens allow the camera to focus on objects at any distance.
E. **Take a Shot:** To capture the image, smoothly press the shutter button the remaining distance.

About Pictures Viewing

Images can be seen on the LCD screen.

❖ Press ▶ to access full-frame images.

You can rotate the front command dial or press the left or right focus stick (focus lever) to view more images. To view images in the order they were recorded, press the focus stick or turn the dial to the right; to view images in the opposite order, turn the dial to the left. To quickly scroll to the chosen frame, keep the focus stick depressed.

Note: A ⊞ ("gift image") indicator is used to indicate that images captured with other cameras might not display properly and that playback zoom might not be accessible.

The HDMI output

Displays used for camera playback and shooting can be broadcast to HDMI devices.

Using HDMI Devices to connect

Use a third-party HDMI cable to connect the camera to TVs or other HDMI devices.
- ❖ Switch off the camera.
- ❖ As indicated below, connect the cable.

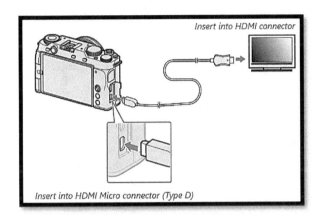

- ❖ Follow the instructions in the device's documentation to set up the device for HDMI input.
- ❖ Activate the camera. The HDMI device will display the contents of the camera display. When in playback mode, the camera's display goes out.
  - Confirming that the connectors are inserted all the way.
  - Make use of an HDMI cable that is no longer than 1.5 meters (4.9 feet).

About Shooting

Movie or live view footage can be saved to an external recorder with an HDMI input or seen on a TV.

The Playback

Press a ▶ button on the camera to begin playback. Pictures and videos are broadcast to the HDMI device when the camera monitor shuts off. Use the television volume controls to alter the volume; the camera volume settings have no influence on TV sounds.

Note: When movie playing starts, some TVs may show a black screen for a brief moment.

Getting Rid of Pictures

The 🗑 button is used to remove images. It is impossible to retrieve deleted images. Before continuing, save key photos or make a copy of them to a computer or other storage device.

❖ Press the 🗑 button and choose [FRAME] when a photo is fully shown.

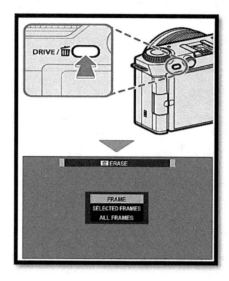

❖ Press the left or right focus stick (focus lever) to navigate among the images, and then select [MENU/OK] to remove them (no confirmation box appears). To remove more images, repeat.
   ▪ It is impossible to remove protected images. If you want to remove a picture, remove its protection.
   ▪ The 🔳 [PLAY BACK MENU] > command can also be used to remove images from menus. [ERASE] choice

How to take Pictures

Selecting a Mode of Shooting

The shutter speed and/or aperture can be changed to select between modes P, S, A, and M. In auto mode (AUTO), you can either manually choose the situation or allow the camera to identify the scene and subject and adjust the settings.

Autofocus

Utilize autofocus when taking pictures.
   ❖ Choose single or continuous AF from the AF/MF SETTING > FOCUS MODE selection in the shooting menu.
   ❖ To choose an AF mode, go to AF/MF SETTING > AF MODE.
   ❖ To change the focus frame's size and location, choose AF/MF SETTING > FOCUS AREA.

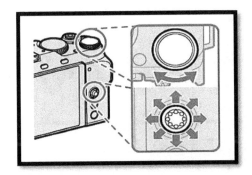

❖ Take pictures.

Making a Focus Point Choice

Use the focus stick (also known as the focus lever) to select the focus point, and use the rear command dial to adjust the focus frame's size. Depending on which AF mode is chosen, the method changes.

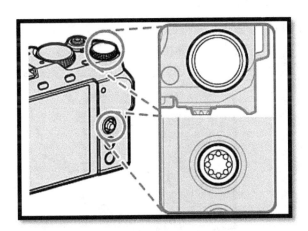

About Autofocus

The following subjects may be difficult for the camera to concentrate on, even with its high-precision autofocus technology.
  ❖ Mirrors and automobile bodywork are examples of glossy objects.
  ❖ Using a window or reflected object to take pictures of subjects.
  ❖ Dark subjects and those with low light reflectance, such fur or hair.
  ❖ Unimportant topics, like fire or smoke.
  ❖ Items that don't stand out against the background.
  ❖ High contrast components, such a subject photo set against a contrasting background, in the focal frame.

Assessing the Focus

Press the center of the rear command dial for perfect focus. To change the focus region, use the focus stick (lever). Press the center of the rear command dial once more to stop the zoom.

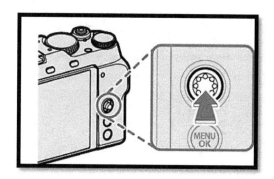

Making Use of Manual Focus

❖ For AF/MF SETTING > FOCUS MODE, select MANUAL FOCUS.
❖ Utilize the lens focus ring to focus manually. You can twist the ring left or right to change the focus distance.

❖ Take a few pictures.

The Quick Focus

❖ Press the focus lock or AF-ON button to start autofocus on a chosen subject.
❖ To rapidly focus on a subject with single or continuous AF in manual focus mode, choose AF/MF SETTING > INSTANT AF SETTING.

Examining the Focus

In manual mode, there are several options for confirming focus.

The Indicator of Manual Focus

The SCREEN SET-UP > FOCUS SCALE UNITS option in the setup menu allows you to adjust the distance to the topic in the focus area in either meters or feet. The depth of field, or the distance in front and behind the object that appears to be in focus, is shown by the blue bar.

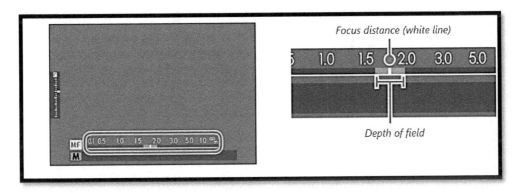

Focus distance (white line)

Depth of field

The depth-of-field indicator can be used to display the manual focus indication in the normal view if both the AF and MF distance indicators are selected under SCREEN SET-UP > DISP. CUSTOM SETTING MENU. Pressing the DISP/BACK button will restore to standard display mode. To modify the depth of field display, select AF/MF SETTING > DEPTH-OF-FIELD SCALE, then select FILM FORMAT BASIS to help you make practical depth of field evaluations for images that will be viewed as prints or similar objects, and PIXEL BASIS to help you make practical depth of field evaluations for images that will be viewed at high resolutions on computers or other electronic displays.

Zoom Focus

If ON is selected under AF/MF SETTING > FOCUS CHECK, the camera will automatically zoom in on the specified focus zone when you turn the focus ring; to leave Zoom, push the center of the rear command dial. The focus stick, often called the focus handle, is used to adjust the focus area. The zoom may be adjusted via the rear command dial. Nevertheless, the zoom cannot be altered when DIGITAL SPLIT IMAGE or DIGITAL MICROPRISM is used for MF aid.

MF Assist

In the photo menus, select AF /MF SETTING > MF ASSIST T. Unlike photos, movies have several focus check settings.

A DIGITAL SPLIT IMAGE

In the center of the frame, there can be a split image. Adjust the focus ring until the divided image's four halves line up correctly. The subject should then be framed inside the split-image area.

A DIGITAL MICROPRISM

The image displays a blurred grid pattern when the subject is out of focus. The grid pattern vanishes when the subject is in focus, revealing a clear image.

FOCUS PEAK HIGHLIGHT

Draws attention to pictures with a lot of contrast. Until the subject is clearly visible, turn the focus ring.

FOCUS METER

A meter appears beneath the focus point display depending on whether the focus is in front of or behind the subject. The needle shifts to the left if the topic is in focus. The subject shifts to the right when the attention is placed behind it. Make sure the needle is pointing straight up by adjusting the focus.

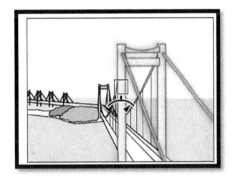

The display flips over when BUTTON/DIAL SETTING > FOCUS RING is rotated CCW.

THE FOCUS MAP

In focus frames, square markers are used to indicate which points, according to their color, are in and out of focus. Both a display that is aimed at the subject and one that is the same distance away from the subject show a green signal. A blue indicator is shown behind the focus position, while a yellow indicator is shown in front of the focus location.

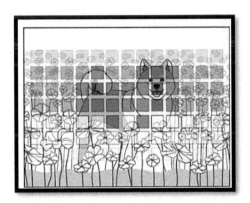

- ❖ In the movie settings, choose AF/MF SETTING > MF ASSIST to convert the sign colors to black and white. This option causes a black indicator to appear behind the focus point and a white indicator to appear in front of it.
- ❖ Autofocus indicators might not be available for challenging subjects.

About Sensitivity

Adjust the camera's sensitivity to light. By raising and rotating the sensitivity slider, you can change the intensity.

- ❖ AUTO1, AUTO2, AUTO3: Depending on the combination of the minimum shutter speed and standard and maximum sensitivity set in SHOOTING SETTING > ISO, sensitivity is automatically modified in response to shooting conditions. AUTO1, AUTO2, and AUTO3 are your options.
- ❖ 125-12800: Manually change the sensitivity. The specified value appears on the display.
- ❖ H (25600/51200), L (64/80/100): Choose for special circumstances. It is important to note that while L restricts dynamic range, mottling may appear in photos produced at H.

Modifying Sensitivity

High values can be utilized to cut down on noise when there is little light. Lower values enable wider apertures or slower shutter speeds in well-lit conditions. Note that there may be mottling in images taken at high sensitivity levels.

Regarding AUTO

For AUTO1, AUTO2, and AUTO3, find the lowest shutter speed, maximum sensitivity, and base sensitivity.

Options

Item	Options
DEFAULT SENSITIVITY	160–12800
MAX. SENSITIVITY	400–12800
MIN. SHUTTER SPEED	1/4000–30 SEC, AUTO

Default

Item	AUTO1	AUTO2	AUTO3
DEFAULT SENSITIVITY	160		
MAX. SENSITIVITY	800	3200	12800
MIN. SHUTTER SPEED	AUTO		

Between the lowest and maximum sensitivity levels, the camera automatically selects one. Only when the value for DEFAULT SENSITIVITY is greater than the value for MAX, or when the minimum shutter speed needed for ideal exposure is less than the value specified for

MIN. SHUTTER SPEED, is the sensitivity changed above the default level. The value chosen for MAX will be used to set SENSITIVITY and DEFAULT SENSITIVITY. SENSITIVITY: If images remain excessively dark at the MAX. If you select AUTO for MIN. SHUTTER SPEED, the camera will automatically select the lowest shutter speed. SENSITIVITY level permits the camera to use slower shutter speeds than MIN. SHUTTER SPEED. Whether or not image stabilization is activated, the minimum shutter speed stays constant.

Metering

Decide how exposure should be measured by the camera. Under SHOOTING SETTING > PHOTOMETRY, you can choose from the following measurement options:
- ❖ In the AF/MF SETTING menu, only one setting will be affected if you select OFF for both FACE/EYE DETECTION SETTING and SUBJECT DETECTION SETTING.
- ❖ **MULTI:** The camera modifies exposure according on color, brightness distribution, and layout. This is generally a wise decision.
- ❖ **CENTER WEIGHTED:** While measuring the full image, the camera focuses on the central region.
- ❖ To measure light in a 2% region of the image, the camera uses SPOT. Suggested for backlit subjects and other scenarios when the background is significantly darker or brighter than the subject.
- ❖ **AVERAGE:** Adjusts exposure to the frame-wide average. For landscape and black-and-white photos of subjects, it offers consistent exposure across several shots with the same illumination, which is highly helpful.
- ❖ Choose AF/MF SETTING > ON to measure the subject in the selected focus area. Interlock Spot and Focus Area AE

Exposure Compensation

Adjust the exposure. Turn the dial for exposure compensation.

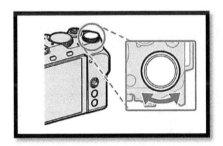

Depending on the shooting mode, different amounts of correction can be applied. Although the shooting display provides an illustration of exposure correction, the effects might not be accurately depicted if
- ❖ The compensation value is greater than ±3 EV.
- ❖ There are two possible settings for the dynamic range: 200 and 400 percent.

❖ Choosing STRONG or WEAK establishes the D RANGE PRIORITY.
You can see how the exposure adjustment will show up on the LCD screen if you press the shutter halfway. The exposure correction results might not display correctly if the camera is in movie mode when F-log is being recorded, or if 200% or 400% DYNAMIC RANGE is selected. By choosing mode M and manually adjusting the exposure, you can obtain an excellent sample.

Focus/Exposure Lock

The shutter button locks exposure and focus when it is pressed halfway.
    ❖ Half-press the shutter while concentrating on the subject to adjust exposure and focus. The focus and exposure will be locked if the shutter button is partially pressed. We refer to this as an AF/AE lock.

    ❖ Fully depress the button.
Only when ON is chosen under BUTTON/DIAL SETTING > SHUTTER AF, SHUTTER AE can the shutter button be used to lock focus and exposure.

The Additional Controls

You may also lock exposure and focus with the AEL and AFON buttons. By default, you can lock exposure without locking focus by pressing the AEL button. Focus but not exposure can be locked with the AFON button set to AF LOCK ONLY.

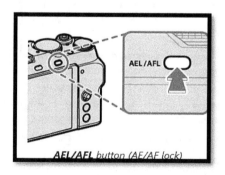

AEL/AFL button (AE/AF lock)

❖ If the designated control is touched while the shutter button is partially tapped, the device will not unlock.

❖ The lock can only be unlocked by pressing the control twice if the AE&AF ON/OFF SWITCH is chosen under BUTTON/DIAL SETTING > AE/AF-LOCK MODE.

During exposure lock, the focus point can be moved using the focus lever (also known as the focus stick). You can assign the AEL and AFON buttons distinct functions by going to BUTTON/DIAL SETTING > FUNCTION (Fn) SETTING. Exposure and focus lock can be controlled by other buttons.

Using bracketing

It will automatically adjust the settings as you view a group of photos.

❖ Press the DRIVE button to bring up drive mode options.

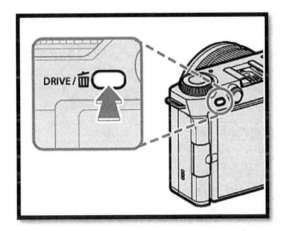

❖ **To highlight any of the following, move the focus stick (also known as the focus lever) up or down:**
  - ISO BKT.
  - BKT White Balance.
  - Bracketing.
❖ The bracketing settings you select can be highlighted by tapping the focus stick left or right.
❖ You can select by tapping MENU/OK.
❖ Take pictures.

The ISO BKT

Select a bracketing amount (±1/3, ±2/3, or ±1) in the drive mode display. The camera will take a picture at the current sensitivity when you release the shutter button, and then process it to make two more copies: one with the sensitivity raised by the predetermined amount, and another with the sensitivity lowered by the same amount.

White Balance BKT

Select the desired amount of bracketing (±1, ±2, or ±3) from the drive mode display. The camera takes a picture when you press the shutter button, then processes it to create three copies: one with the white balance setting as it is, one with fine-tuning increased by the amount you choose, and one with fine-tuning decreased by the amount you choose. Subsequently, it generates two further copies, one with the sensitivity raised by the amount you chose and the other with the sensitivity lowered by it.

Bracketing for BKT

AE BKT

Go to SHOOTING SETTING > AE BKT SETTING to change the number of shots, bracketing quantity, and bracketing order. The camera will take the number of consecutive shots you specify, using the measured exposure value for the first shot and multiples of the amount you choose for bracketing to over- or under-expose the subsequent shots. No matter how much bracketing is employed, the exposure will not go beyond the limitations of the exposure measurement method.

BKT FILM SIMULATION

You can adjust the film simulation settings by navigating to SHOOTING SETTING > FILM SIMULATION BKT. The camera takes a picture when you press the shutter button, then processes it to create copies with various parameters.

BKT DYNAMIC RANGE

The camera captures three images with different dynamic ranges when you push the shutter button: 100%, 200%, and 400%. The sensitivity will be restricted to ISO 640 or above when dynamic range bracketing is activated. Sensitivity reverts to its initial value when bracketing is stopped.

FOCUS BKT

The shutter button causes the camera to take a sequence of pictures, each with its own focus. There are two bracket options under SHOOTING SETTING > FOCUS BKT SETTING: MANUAL and AUTO.
   ❖ When shooting, avoid altering the zoom.
   ❖ It is recommended to use a tripod.

Continuous shooting (burst mode)

Record motion in a series of pictures

- ❖ To enter the drive mode menu, press the DRIVE button. From there, choose either CL LOW-SPEED BURST or CH HIGH-SPEED BURST.
- ❖ To start shooting, choose the frame advance rate and press the shutter button.

Attention:
- Release the shutter button to cease shooting once the memory card is full.
- The remaining images will be stored in a new folder if the file count above 9999 before shooting concludes.
- Until the memory card is full, the camera will continue to store pictures. Burst shooting might not begin if the memory card has inadequate capacity.
- Frame rates may decrease as more pictures are taken.
- The frame rate varies based on the sensitivity, shutter speed, and focus mode.
- Depending on the shooting conditions, the flash may not work properly or frame rates may slow.
- Longer recording periods could result from faster filming.
- The SHOOTING SETTING > SHUTTER TYPE selection determines the different burst kinds.

About HDR

The camera captures three images with varying exposures when the shutter button is pressed. After that, these photos are combined to create a single picture. Both the highlights and the shadows' attributes were used to produce the image.
- ❖ Tap the DRIVE button to bring up the drive-mode options and choose HDR.
- ❖ Decide how much the brightness of the exposures changes.
- ❖ Take pictures.
  - A blended image will be produced by the camera.

Take note:
- Make sure the camera doesn't move.
- Modifying the setup, lighting, or subject during filming could have unfavorable effects.
- The quality of the photograph will be reduced because just a little portion will be deleted.
- Photographs taken at a higher level may show mottling. Pick a number that makes sense in the given circumstance.
- There is no support for extended sensitivity settings.
- Images may not be taken at the required shutter speed, depending on the sensitivity and HDR settings.
- The flash does not turn on.

Panoramas

❖ Select PANORAMA from the drive mode options that appear after pressing the DRIVE button.
❖ Press the focus stick (focus lever) to the left to adjust the angle at which you will pan the camera while filming. After highlighting a size, choose MENU/OK.
❖ Use the focus stick on the right to see a range of pan directions. After selecting a pan direction, press MENU/OK.
❖ Press the shutter button all the way down to begin recording. It is not necessary to hold down the shutter button during the recording.
❖ Move the camera in the arrow's specified direction. The shooting procedure ends automatically when the camera reaches the end of the guides and the panorama is finished.

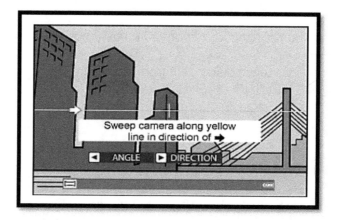

For Optimal Outcomes
❖ Slowly and steadily move the camera in a tiny circle.
❖ Only pan in the direction specified by the instructions, and position the camera parallel to or at right angles to the horizon.
❖ Try other panning speeds if the intended outcomes are not achieved.
❖ Keep your elbows close to your sides.
❖ Make use of a tripod.
❖ Use a lens with a focal length of 35 mm or less (50 mm in 35 mm format) for best results.

The shooting will stop and no panorama will be recorded if you press the shutter button all the way down before the panorama is complete. The last segment might not be captured if filming ends before the panorama is completed. The camera may not always be able to accurately stitch together the many frames that make up a panorama. Insufficient illumination of the topic might cause panoramas to appear fuzzy. If the camera is panned too quickly or too slowly, shooting may stop. The filming is stopped if the camera is panned in a different direction from the one displayed. Rarely, the camera might capture an angle that differs from the designated one.

The expected results might not be achieved with:

- ❖ Subjects in motion.
- ❖ People close to the camera.
- ❖ Things that never change, like the sky or a field of grass.
- ❖ Things that are always moving, like waterfalls and waves.
- ❖ Individuals exhibiting notable variations in brightness.

Multiple exposures

Make a picture with several exposures

- ❖ **Select a blend mode:** Take the first shot. Tap the DRIVE button to bring up the drive mode options, and then select MULTIPLE EXPOSURE.
- ❖ When you tap MENU/OK, the first picture will appear over the view through the lens, requesting that you take a second picture.
  - ▪ Tap the focus stick to the left to go back to the original shot point.
  - ▪ Press DISP/BACK to maintain the original image and prevent additional exposures.
- ❖ Using the first frame as a guide, take another picture.

Press MENU/OK

- ❖ **The subsequent picture will be arranged using the combined exposures as a guide.**
  - ▪ Press the focus stick to the left to go back to the first step and try the second shot again.
  - ▪ To halt shooting and generate numerous exposures from earlier images, press DISP/BACK.

Create additional exposures

- ❖ Up to nine exposures are possible for each photograph.
- ❖ Use the DISP/BACK key to get out of the shooting mode.
- ❖ After shooting with many exposures, the camera will provide a combined image.
- ❖ If ISO sensitivity is assigned to the front command dial function, you can change the sensitivity of AUTO1, AUTO2, or AUTO3 by setting the auto mode selector lever to AUTO.

CHAPTER FIVE

FLASH SETTING (FOR STILL PHOTOGRAPHY)

Modify flash-related parameters for still photographs

In the photo shooting display, press [MENU/OK] and choose the ⚡ ([FLASH SETTING]) tab to view the flash settings.

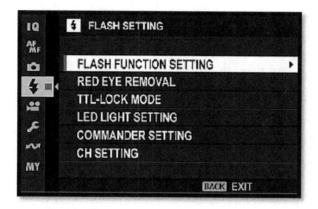

❖ [FLASH FUNCTION SETTING]
❖ [RED EYE REMOVAL]
❖ [TTL-LOCK MODE]
❖ [LED LIGHT SETTING]
❖ [COMMANDER SETTING]
❖ [CH SETTING]

[FLASH FUNCTION SETTING]

You can change the flash level or select a flash control, flash, or sync mode. Depending on the flash, different alternatives are available.

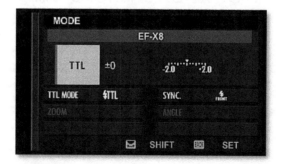

The flash output power/compensation amount, flash control mode, flash mode, and sync mode can all be selected from this menu. Depending on the flash you're using, your options will vary, but they're rather simple.

You'll easily figure it out if you try it a few times.
- ❖ The TTL, Manual, Commander, and Off flash control modes are available. Commander mode allows you to control remote flash units that are not connected to your camera using the flash on your camera.
- ❖ **FLASH COMPENSATION/OUTPUT:** Modify output and flash compensation settings.
- ❖ **FLASH MODE (TTL):** To modify the TTL, choose a flash mode (TTL). The choices you have depend on whether you are using the P, S, A, or M exposure shooting modes.
- ❖ **FLASH AUTO:** This feature modifies output according to the brightness of the subject. The flash will turn on when you press the shutter halfway down and the LCD panel displays the tiny "lightning bolt" symbol.
- ❖ **STANDARD:** Every shot will, if at all feasible, trigger the flash. The brightness of the scene affects how much flash is used. The flash won't turn on when you hit the shutter until it is completely charged.
- ❖ **SLOW SYNC:** To achieve the well-liked fuzzy motion look, use slow shutter speeds with the flash. The slow-shutter flash appeals to me. Take action. You'll find it entertaining. Slow shutter sync flash is what I always use. A lot of experts do.
- ❖ **SYNC:** Controls the flash's ignition time.
- ❖ **Front/1st CURTAIN:** Opening the shutter causes the flash to turn on.
- ❖ **REAR/2nd CURTAIN:** Just prior to the shutter closing, the flash fires. The greatest and most advised method for taking practically any kind of flash photo is this one. It looks great when used with a SLOW SYNC flash.

Your flash should be set to REAR CURTAIN, in my opinion.

[RED EYE REMOVAL]

Get rid of the flash's red-eye effects.

Option	Description
[FLASH]	Flash red-eye reduction only.
[OFF]	Flash red-eye reduction and digital red-eye removal off.

Note: TTL flash control mode allows for the usage of flash red-eye reduction.

[TTL-LOCK MODE]

It is possible to lock TTL flash control to maintain consistent effects across several images. You won't need to adjust the flash intensity for every picture this way. **There are two options available to you here.**

Option	Description
[LOCK WITH LAST FLASH]	Flash output is locked at the value metered for the most recent photo.
[LOCK WITH METERING FLASH]	The camera emits a series of pre-flashes and locks flash output at the metered value.

This feature is particularly useful since it maintains the same illumination in each picture, thereby prolonging the life of your flash battery. Set TTL-LOCK if the light doesn't change. It is possible to connect TTL-LOCK to a Fn button and use it to turn it on and off.

Design note:

❖ Assigning [TTL-LOCK] to a camera control and using it to activate or disable TTL lock is how TTL lock is used.
❖ During TTL lock, flash compensation may be changed.
❖ An error notice appears if there isn't a previously metered value when you choose [LOCK WITH LAST FLASH].

[LED LIGHT SETTING]

When shooting pictures, you may choose to utilize the LED video light on the flash unit (if it's available) as an AF-assist illuminator or as a catchlight.

Option	Role of LED video light in still photography
[CATCHLIGHT]	Catchlight
[AF ASSIST]	AF-assist illuminator
[AF ASSIST+CATCHLIGHT]	AF-assist illuminator and catchlight
[OFF]	None

Note: In some situations, the [FLASH FUNCTION SETTING] menu may also be used to access this option.

[COMMANDER SETTING]

For Fujifilm optical wireless remote flash control, choose groups when using the camera flash unit as a commander. When the camera is used with clip-on flash units that enable Fujifilm optical wireless flash control, this option becomes accessible.

Options			
[Gr A]	[Gr B]	[Gr C]	[OFF]

Note: This option may also be accessible through the [FLASH FUNCTION SETTING] menu in certain circumstances.

[CH SETTING]

Select the channel that the commander and remote flash units will use to communicate. When many flash systems are functioning in close proximity to one another, separate channels might be utilized for each system or to avoid interference. There are four choices available for communicating between the master and remote units utilizing a FUJIFILM flash with optical wireless flash control.

Options			
[CH1]	[CH2]	[CH3]	[CH4]

CHAPTER SIX

ABOUT IMAGE QUALITY SETTINGS (SHOOTING MENU)

Modify the picture quality settings for still photos. Select the (IMAGE QUALITY SETTING) tab after selecting MENU/OK on the picture shooting display to see the image quality options.

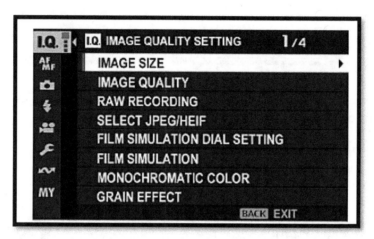

Depending on the shooting mode used, several options are available.

- ❖ IMAGE SIZE
- ❖ IMAGE QUALITY
- ❖ RAW RECORDING
- ❖ SELECT JPEG/HEIF
- ❖ FILM SIMULATION DIAL SETTING
- ❖ FILM SIMULATION
- ❖ MONOCHROMATIC COLOR
- ❖ GRAIN EFFECT
- ❖ COLOR CHROME EFFECT
- ❖ COLOR CHROME FX BLUE
- ❖ WHITE BALANCE
- ❖ DYNAMIC RANGE
- ❖ D RANGE PRIORITY
- ❖ TONE CURVE
- ❖ COLOR
- ❖ SHARPNESS
- ❖ HIGH ISO NR
- ❖ CLARITY
- ❖ LONG EXPOSURE NR
- ❖ LONG EXPOSURE NR
- ❖ LENS MODULATION OPTIMIZER

❖ COLOR SPACE
❖ PIXEL MAPPING
❖ EDIT/SAVE CUSTOM SETTING
❖ AUTO UPDATE CUSTOM SETTING
❖ CUSTOM MODE SETTING
❖ MOUNT ADAPTOR SETTING

The MY MENU cameras' first menu is called Image Quality Setting. You may alter the appearance and feel of your photographs using this option. The IMAGE QUALITY SETTINGS menu has a number of rather extensive choices. They take up about three pages. You'll discover that you use RAW recording, white balance, image size, quality, film simulations, and maybe highlight tone, shadow tone, and custom settings the most. Keep in mind that each of these items is already connected to a Q menu position or a Fn button. The RED and Q menus provide access to the majority of these options for the RED/BLUE versions.

Image Size and Quality

Let's examine Image Size and Image Quality, the first two menu options.

Image Size

S, M, and L are the three different sizes or aspect ratios that the camera can shoot in. Keep in mind that they only work with JPEG files. You will only be shooting in RAW and the file will be full-size if you do not use this option. Photographs may still be altered in terms of aspect ratio and size.

Option (Image size)	
L 3:2 (6240 × 4160)	**L** 1:1 (4160 × 4160)
L 16:9 (6240 × 3512)	
M 3:2 (4416 × 2944)	**M** 1:1 (2944 × 2944)
M 16:9 (4416 × 2488)	
S 3:2 (3120 × 2080)	**S** 1:1 (2080 × 2080)
S 16:9 (3120 × 1760)	

The following choices show up when you choose 1.29X CROP in SPORTS FINDER MODE or burst mode.

Option (Image size)	
M 3:2 (4992 × 3328)	**M** 1:1 (3328 × 3328)
M 16:9 (4992 × 2808)	

L3:2 provides me the greatest space, therefore that's where I usually shoot. However, shooting 3:2 is not required by any regulation. I can choose to photograph a 1:1 square picture or a widescreen 16:9 image for my creative viewpoint and subject matter. Changes in aspect ratio may sometimes be enjoyable. You may use a different aspect ratio, such 1:1, while shooting RAW+JPEG without compromising quality. You will have a RAW file that contains all of the data from the whole sensor, even if your JPEG will be square. The maximum resolution, which is 6000 x 4000 pixels for 24MP sensor cameras and 4896 x 3264 pixels for 16MP sensor cameras, is what I often recommend. Both memory and card space are of excellent quality and are reasonably priced. Nonetheless, there are certain situations when it would be better to shoot in smaller volumes. A little 3MB file will suffice if all you want to do is view your photos on a computer and don't want to use up too much space. This size (3008 × 2000 pixels) can fit on most computer screens and is appropriate for a 5 x 8-inch picture. But remembering is cheap, as I said before, and you never know what you'll achieve with your photos or whether you'll get a special one. What if you manage to get a picture of Nessie or Bigfoot? Full resolution should have been used while taking the picture.

Image Quality

Option	Description
[FINE]	Low compression ratios are used for higher-quality images.
[NORMAL]	Higher compression ratios are used to increase the number of images that can be stored.
[FINE+RAW]	Record both RAW and fine-quality JPEG or HEIF images.
[NORMAL+RAW]	Record both RAW and normal-quality JPEG or HEIF images.
[RAW]	Record RAW images only.

Both RAW and JPEG files may be saved with this camera. To capture RAW pictures, choose RAW; to capture JPEG images, select FINE or NORMAL; or to capture both RAW and JPEG images, select (RAW)F or (RAW)N. RAW+JPEG is the typical name for this mode. JPEG images get better quality when compressed with FINE or RAW. The quantity of photographs that may fit on your memory card is increased when you choose NORMAL or RAW compression, but the quality is somewhat diminished. I suggest FINE if you're shooting JPEGs. These photographs are reasonably priced and of good quality, even if they need more memory card capacity. Keep in mind that if you shoot RAW+JPEG, the JPEG is the only one that is impacted by the FINE or NORMAL picture quality settings.

When to take pictures in RAW, JPEG, or RAW+JPEG

Let's examine the many methods for capturing RAW files, JPEGs, or both.

The JPEG

When you photograph in JPEG mode, what happens? The image processor in the camera converts the file into a picture after evaluating all of the exposure data from the sensor and applying your current image quality settings. When you play it back, you see the picture that was saved on your memory card. In order to produce a high-quality picture with a manageable file size, the camera makes decisions about which data to retain and which to discard throughout the distillation process. You will lose information that cannot be recovered when you open your JPEG picture using any application. Since FUJIFILM image processors read data very well and almost always produce high-quality photographs, this is often not a problem. However, when photographing situations with exceptionally brilliant highlights and extremely dark blacks, the camera may not be able to capture all of your data because of the way the image processor creates a JPEG. Even if the finished picture looks excellent, trying to fix the harsh tones in Photoshop can just make things worse since you won't be able to obtain the information you need.

RAW

Instead of capturing a "image" when you shoot in RAW, the camera transmits all of the exposure data from the sensor to the memory card as raw data, exposing the settings you were using at the time. Because RAW files include a lot of data, they are quite large. Instead of a RAW file, you will see a processed JPEG when you look at the back of the camera. During the shooting process, the camera also manages the file, creating a medium-sized JPEG preview that is saved with the RAW data. You may now see your picture on the LCD thanks to this. Because a RAW file contains all of the sensor's original data, you have a far higher chance of maintaining, recovering, and modifying the colors and tones when processing the picture with your preferred photo program. Compared to a JPEG, a RAW file permits a lot more errors. A photograph does not always get better just because it was taken in RAW. Because the Fuji JPEGs are ready to use straight out of the camera, there's no need to spend time processing them, and they usually look fantastic. You will need to work to restore the RAW data as they were on the back of the camera when you shot the picture since most programs will load and save them with a "flat" color profile and without the Film Simulation you selected. By letting the camera handle image processing, you may save time and get better-looking photos than you would if you did it yourself. Additionally, your photos will take up less space on your card or computer. Use the built-in RAW CONVERSION function to convert RAW images to JPEGs.

RAW+JPEG

Both the RAW file and the altered JPEG are stored on the memory card when this mode is employed. Although the JPEG image will probably look fantastic straight out of the camera, you will also have the RAW file in case you wish to make any further changes. Another advantage is that shooting in this mode maintains your Film Simulation. As mentioned earlier, Adobe substitutes their standard, flat Adobe color profile for the Fuji Film Simulation when you import RAW files into Lightroom or Photoshop. The colors will be lost when you import the file into Lightroom if you choose one of the film simulations but only shoot in RAW. You may use them again under the Camera Calibration tab of Lightroom or Photoshop, but keep in mind that these are Adobe's rendition of the Fuji film sim color profiles, and while they are excellent, they don't quite match the film sims that came with the camera. The RAW file will act as your "digital negative." You will typically not need the RAW file, and it will probably only take up space on your hard drive. If you shoot RAW+JPEG, you will receive a JPEG that looks exactly like the photo you took, which you can then post, email, share, or transfer to your phone. You may want to save the RAW file, however, if you're shooting for a client or in low light. The bride did not like the hue of any of the wedding photos my friend took with her Fuji camera. By returning to the RAW files, my buddy was able to change the colors. I shoot in JPEG mode most of the time, but if I need a RAW file, I always shoot in RAW+JPEG mode instead of RAW just.

The Function Buttons

Assign RAW picture quality to a function button to enable or deactivate it for a single shot. To choose an option from the right column, press the button once. To go back to the original setup (left column), press the button again.

Option currently selected for IMAGE QUALITY	Option selected by pressing function button to which RAW is assigned
FINE	FINE+RAW
NORMAL	NORMAL+RAW
FINE+RAW	FINE
NORMAL+RAW	NORMAL
RAW	FINE

RAW RECORDING

❖ There are two options for recording RAW files in the MY MENU mode: if UNCOMPRESSED is selected, the RAW file won't be compressed.

❖ LOSSLESS COMPRESSED uses reverse compression to reduce file size without sacrificing quality when saving RAW files. Because they are so big, they occupy a lot more space on your card. An X-T2 RAW file is around 50MB in size when it is not compressed. In contrast, a Lossless Compressed file is between 25 and 35 megabytes in size.

❖ **COMPRESSED:** A "lossy," irreversible method is used to compress RAW images. Although the files are typically 25 to 35 percent less than the uncompressed size, the picture quality is equal to UNCOMPRESSED.

❖ Lossless Compressed conserves card space without sacrificing quality. What makes the Uncompressed option available, then? If this option was not available, the camera would probably not be bought by the few real pixel peepers who think it makes a difference.

I think everyone else should simply forget about it and set their cameras to LOSSLESS COMPRESSED.

SELECT JPEG/HEIF

The JPEG and HEIF picture formats are available for you to choose from.

❖ One popular image format for storing pictures is JPEG.

❖ Although the HEIF format reduces viewing and sharing possibilities, it compresses data.

In Du Ring Multiple Exposure Graphs, JPEG is instantly favored over HEIF. The COLOR SPACE is set to sRGB and CLARITY is turned off when you choose HEIF. Heif photos are saved on memory cards as files with the extension ".HIF," which need to be changed to ".HEIC" in order to be viewed on a computer. This happens automatically when HEIF photos are sent from a camera to a computer using USB.

FILM SIMULATION DIAL SETTING

You may alter the film simulations and filters by setting the film simulation dial to FS1, FS2, FS3, or ACROS.

FS1, FS2, and FS3

Choose the desired film simulation for FS1, FS2, and FS3 on the film simulation dial. Choose either MONOCHROME or ACROS as your filter.

ACROS

Use a filter when the film simulation dial is set to ACROS.

FILM SIMULATIONS

Try with several film effects, such black and white (with or without color filters), and choose a color scheme that complements your topic and creative objectives. The options and descriptions are as follows:

AUTO

The camera will automatically choose the optimal film simulation mode for the situation when the auto mode selection lever is set to AUTO.

PROVIA/STANDARD

PROVIA, a film created from a professional ISO 100 slide film, is the default option. It is appropriate for a variety of subject matter because to its excellent color reproduction, medium sharpness, and reasonable tonal balance. It may be used with almost any light and topic, making it the "jack of all trades" among cinema simulations.

VELVIA/VIVID

With its very rich color, extremely saturated color spectrum, and inky black shadows, Fuji picture Film (as they were once called) revolutionized picture photography in 1991 with the advent of an ISO 50 color reversal (slide) film. VELVIA quickly became the preferred film for adventure, wildlife, travel, and scenic fans across the globe because it was perfect for outdoor photographers. Because of how accurate the colors are, VELVIA, which stands for "Velvet Media," or "bright," was my favorite slide film and is now my favorite film simulation. For the majority of outdoor photos, it does a great job of capturing the enthusiasm and confidence of your subjects; however it's not always accurate or true to reality.

Actually, when Fuji's color experts created the original VELVIA color profile, they added a bit of magenta to the blue tones, adding depth and flavor to the blue sky and making it more "memorable." Humans tend to remember colors, events, and relationships as "enhanced" compared to their real-life counterparts. VELVIA plays with this psychological component of memory and helps photojournalists create images that stay in the minds of our viewers. When we look at a picture of a beautiful scene that is extremely true to reality, we feel that it is "missing something." If you prefer deep shadows and vivid colors, VELVIA is the film simulation for you—but only on sunny days. Bright blue skies, green grass or foliage, bright red and orange flowers, bags, tents, motorcycles, coats, and pretty much everything else you can think of are all perfect. However, unless you're shooting up close, VELVIA doesn't look well in dark or even bright conditions. People with darker complexion should not wear it since it has too many contrasts and tones for gloomy backdrops and dark sky.

ASTIA/SOFT

ASTIA is ideal for taking pictures of people outdoors during the day since it is based on Fuji's professional ISO 100 color reversal portrait and fashion film, which blends nicely with skin tones and clothing. However, since the color is vivid and does not wane as the image's contrast rises, it looks fantastic on any subject, inside or out. I find ASTIA useful for a variety of locations and themes, which is why I use it as my go-to film simulator on cloudy days when VELVIA is too bright.

The word "SOFT" in the title of the movie game shouldn't be deceptive; ASTIA is meant to gently smooth skin tones, but it also makes dark tones harder to balance and sharpens your photos.

CLASSIC CHROME

Because CLASSIC CHROME is not as bright as other film simulations, the colors are softer and the visuals seem better. Although Fuji cannot rightfully refer to it as Kodachrome, the most common film material, CLASSIC CHROME was designed to look like it. When compared to VELVIA, CLASSIC CHROME may seem dull at first, but once you know what it does, you'll see that it produces a really amazing, almost monochromatic effect (but in color). CLASSIC CHROME has an interesting sound; the highlights are gentle, but the shadows are rougher, suggesting that it may be used for shooting under cloudy skies. The brighter tones do not fade as quickly, but it becomes a little deeper in the shadows, which you may use in a number of situations. It is similar to VELVIA in reverse, drawing the viewer's eye to a scene's structure and tone instead of its color scheme. It's ideal for street photography, reportage, and natural portraiture because the subject—rather than the colors—is the primary emphasis.

REALA ACE

For photographers who want to quickly and effectively capture the essence of their subjects, REALA ACE is a versatile substitute. It is advised to choose this setting in order to capture a variety of images clearly and vividly.

Pro Neg Hi and Std

Fuji's popular NPS 160 print film, which was the go-to film for wedding and portrait photographers, is the basis for both PRO Neg film simulations. The FinePix 700 digital camera was the first to employ them in 2004. Because PRO Neg Hi has more color than Std, the contrast is higher. There isn't a better approach to photograph city scenes or the outdoors. Of all the film simulations, PRO Neg Std has the lowest tonality, resulting in images with soft, flat colors and minimal contrast, although skin tones are more realistic. It is intended to provide the best results when employing studio lighting and flash for interior photography. I often utilize these two simulators since I really love shooting with them.

CLASSIC Neg.

This option enhances color rendering and gives photos a strong tone, making it ideal for creating bright, sharp images in a variety of circumstances.

Nostalgic Neg.

This gives the highlights a hint of orange and brings out the dark tones, making the picture seem like it was printed. Warm tones that arouse memories give images a timeless appeal.

ETERNA/CINEMA

This option offers a classic cinematic aesthetic for giving still and moving images a cinematic feel. It produces deep shadows and gentle hues, much as in movies.

ETERNA BLEACH BYPASS

As a result, combining low brightness and high contrast creates a unique artistic style that infuses both photos and films with a dash of creativity and energy. Both still photography and motion pictures may use this approach.

ACROS

The X-Pro2 was the first platform to run the black-and-white film simulation known as ACROS. Compared to conventional black-and-white simulations, it requires more processing resources because to its intricate grain structure and high degree of color. It has red (R), green (G), and yellow (Ye) filters that deepen grays by matching colors that go well with the color you choose.

- **ACROS+Ye FILTER** enhances contrast and darkens clouds.
- **ACROS+R FILTER** enhances contrast and darkens clouds.
- **ACROS+G FILTER:** Enhances skin tones in portraiture.

A picture with a lot of depth and tonal gradation is produced by ACROS's tonality curve, which can preserve information in both bright whites and deep shadows. In addition, it creates a lovely, distinctive quantity of grain that looks like film grain. ACROS resembles a black-and-white picture, with more grain in the darker areas and almost none in the bright ones. The higher the ISO dial is set, the stronger the grit. At ISO 3200, ACROS produces stunning images with lovely tones and film-like texture. Some images maintain a great degree of clarity at ISO 12800, and the grain seems to be the same as in a Kodak T-MAX 3200 print. If you have a later Fuji, shoot with the ACROS film emulation, but don't be afraid to shoot at any ISO. I often shoot at ISO 3200 during the day to get that beautiful grain. Keep in mind that the goal of photography is to capture reality, thus some grain is OK.

MONOCHROME

If your camera lacks ACROS, you may use MONOCHROME as a black-and-white film emulation. I'm grateful that it's compatible with all X Series cameras. Don't worry about what you're missing out on if you don't have ACROS since MONOCHROME is an amazing movie emulator that you will love. You may even use the previously stated Ye, R, and G color filter options.

- MONOCHROME+YE FILTER: Improves contrast and darkens clouds.
- MONOCHROME+R FILTER: Improves contrast and darkens clouds.
- MONOCHROME+G FILTER: Enhances skin tones in portraiture.

The SEPIA

It is very antiquated and easy to grasp. Like in very old photographs, it's brighter and has a distinct brownish-yellow tint, similar to black and white. Although you won't use it much, you may find it entertaining sometimes.

COLOR MONOCHROMATIC

Use the WARM and COOL axes in addition to the G and M axes to alter the color cast of the ACROS and MONOCHROME film models.

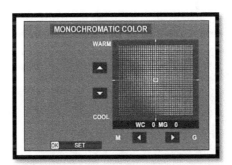

GRAIN EFFECT

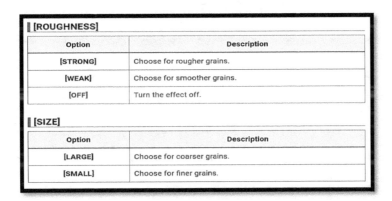

[ROUGHNESS]

Option	Description
[STRONG]	Choose for rougher grains.
[WEAK]	Choose for smoother grains.
[OFF]	Turn the effect off.

[SIZE]

Option	Description
[LARGE]	Choose for coarser grains.
[SMALL]	Choose for finer grains.

There are three possibilities for this setting: strong, weak, and off. It gives your photos a "film grain" look. I am aware that some professional photographers may be offended by this choice, but it can also be enjoyable. As I said before, great photography portrays what it is intended to portray. A major factor in the fact that many of us recall photography as a form of creative expression is grain, which is present in many of our images. Here's what I just said: a little grain doesn't hurt anybody, and it could even provide a unique look to certain photos that you like. This option is useful in the situation. Why don't I just increase the ISO level to acquire grain? I get your reasoning. Using the GRAIN EFFECT option will give color high ISO photos a more pronounced grain layer, giving them a more film-like appearance. This is compatible with the ACROS Film Simulation and may be done at high ISO levels. Your features will last a little longer when you use grain at low ISO settings than when you use really high ISO settings. For instance, fine details will be quite visible at ISO 200, and they will be accompanied by a smooth grain. However, the noise (grain) will be a bit mushier and the fine details will be less noticeable at ISO 6400 and 12800. Whether you want to employ GRAIN EFFECT or not is up to you; you may choose not to use it.

COLOR CHROME EFFECT

Expand the range of tones that may be used to depict colors that are prone to being very bright, such as reds, yellows, and greens.

Option	Description
[STRONG]	Choose for a strong effect.
[WEAK]	Choose for a weak effect.
[OFF]	Turn the effect off.

COLOR BLUE CHROME FX

To generate blues, more tones have to be available.

Option	Description
[STRONG]	Choose for a strong effect.
[WEAK]	Choose for a weak effect.
[OFF]	Turn the effect off.

SMOOTH SKIN EFFECT

Smooth complexions

Option	Description
[STRONG]	Choose for a strong effect.
[WEAK]	Choose for a weak effect.
[OFF]	Turn the effect off.

A WHITE BALANCE

Every kind of light has a distinct color temperature based on the Kelvin scale. White light, like to that of the sun or an electric flash, is produced at 5,000 degrees K. Temperatures in the blue range are higher and blue hues are warmer than red. The light from an orange sunset may be about 2,900 degrees Kelvin, to give you an idea. Additionally, different kinds of artificial lighting have different effects on the hues. The yellow light that sodium vapor lamps generate is one characteristic that sets them apart from fluorescent lights. Incandescent lights are orange. Because our brains "fix" the hue of light to make it seem more neutral, our eyes are unable to detect this. Our eyes have evolved over time to enable precise color detection and identification in a variety of lighting conditions. Since the camera's brain adjusts white balance instead of digital sensors, the majority of cameras, including the X Series models, feature many WHITE BALANCE (WB) options in addition to AUTO white balance. You may also make manual modifications with them. As shown below, it features a variety of white balance options. Keep in mind that the white balance you choose while shooting in JPEG will be permanently preserved in the picture. The white balance will be preset if you're shooting RAW, but you may always adjust it in your picture software.

Auto-White Priority

There are many uses for this tool, which instantly changes the white balance of your camera. It is quite beneficial when the setting seems warm and bright due to the use of incandescent lights. This feature adds weight to lighter whites in your photos to make the colors seem as natural as possible. This puts in a lot of effort behind the scenes to maintain the colors, so whether you're outdoors in a range of lighting conditions or at home with artificial lighting, you can capture moments with authenticity and clarity.

The AUTO option

The AUTO option adjusts the white balance automatically, which often works well. This is very amazing when you consider it. You're photographing a stunning sunset with a lot of orange light. Although this photograph would technically have a rather warm white balance, it would not look well if the camera was set to this temperature; you want to preserve the beautiful orange light in the picture. The camera's WB light meter and algorithms make the scenario seem normal when you choose AUTO white balance. The WB will sometimes make small adjustments even if the light stays the same. I had this thought at sunset. Now is the moment to pay more attention to what your LCD panel appears excellent than to what is correct. I moved the camera a little bit and changed the white balance to take pictures at sunset. I just adjust the camera till I get the desired look. I then recompose after locking the exposure by halfway lowering the shutter. One of my favorite images from the Great Smoky Mountains is this one. The picture below shows a quite erratic appearance. The second picture looked quite different from the first because of minor adjustments made to the camera's white balance.

Tap OK on any setting, including AUTO, to adjust the white balance. Using the joystick or thumb pad buttons, move the mouse along the Red, Green, and Blue axes to change the scene's color. The WB SHIFT color grid will appear as a result. Once you're happy with the look, click OK once again. Remember that until you adjust it again, this white balance setting will remain on your camera. Usually, this is what causes odd color casts in photos. Verify whether the White Balance setting has been altered. Usually, I choose AUTO for the white balance on my camera, and the pictures come out OK.

Auto AMBIENCE PRIORITY

Your camera's white balance will be quickly adjusted, which is a helpful feature. Incandescent lights are particularly useful in areas with adequate illumination since they provide a brighter light. By prioritizing warmer whites, this option ensures that your photos faithfully convey the local ambiance. Whether you're photographing cozy moments in the glory of a sunset or inside with gentle, warm lighting, you can choose Auto AMBIENCE PRIORITY to preserve the scene's inherent warmth. With the aid of this feature, you may take pictures that make you feel comfortable and at home by capturing the tone and ambiance of your surroundings.

Customs 1, 2, and 3

Three unique WB settings may be saved. After selecting your preferred slot, hit the fun stick or OK. By selecting this option, you may snap a picture and have the camera adjust the white balance to match the lighting in the surrounding area. "Completed!" will show up when the picture has been taken. Select OK to accept the new WB; press BACK to withdraw. To get the RGB WB SHIFT option, press OK one more rather than taking a picture. Click OK once more after selecting your favorite hue, and it will save there. If you want the camera to show a scene or kind of lighting in a slightly different manner, this is an excellent alternative. You most likely believe that nighttime images are too green and dismal situations are too blue. To make your surroundings more vibrant, you could also want to use fuchsia. A hint of fuchsia is used into VELVIA's color palette to accentuate the blues. For instance, you may create a custom white balance if you often take pictures inside in a certain kind of artificial light. You may change the WB and save it as a favorite, or you can choose from a range of WB settings, such SHADE or CLOUDY. I've lightened situations with plenty of shadows by using this option.

The color temperature

You may choose your color temperature in degrees Kelvin when using this white balance option. The higher-level settings will provide warmth to make up for unusually chilly illumination. Similarly, using lower settings can make your scene cooler if it's too warm. Imagine that AUTO isn't quite getting it right while you're taking a picture under artificial light. Choose the K option and input the exact color temperature to get the desired skin tones. Feel free to play around with this configuration. Even if the picture does not seem to be the genuine thing, the K scale may be altered to make it warmer or cooler.

Daylight

This choice is appropriate for situations that come up throughout the day. When shooting in bright, sunny conditions, I know photographers who prefer this over AUTO. Usually, the white balance is quite close. Under various lighting conditions, AUTO will seem somewhat different. For instance, it provides a hint of pink when the light is hazy. Try this one out and see what you like most, in my opinion.

Shade

This option will add yellow to warm up the picture and make the colors seem as they would in daylight since shaded settings have a pronounced blue tint. while AUTO isn't just perfect, I always go for SHADE while photographing in dim or overcast conditions. The scene captured with AUTO white balance is seen in the first picture below. The exact incident captured using the SHADE setting is seen in the second picture. They seem to be significantly different when placed close to one another. The first is distinctly blue in color. The second one seems to be almost brown. The second picture seems to have a more balanced color tone when examined alone. Do you understand? The viewer may be deceived by color when comparing two photos side by side.

FLUORESCENT LIGHT-1, and FLUORESCENT LIGHT-2, as well as FLUORESCENT LIGHT-3

These are certain settings that help the white balance function at its peak in various bright light conditions.

- ❖ FLUORESCENT LIGHT-1 is suitable for environments with "daylight" fluorescent lighting as it ensures accurate color reproduction.
- ❖ FLUORESCENT LIGHT-2 creates softer tones by altering white balance to resemble "warm white" fluorescent lights.
- ❖ Accurate color representation in cooler tones is ensured by the FLUORESCENT LIGHT-3's design for "cool white" fluorescent lights.

By choosing the appropriate fluorescent light setting for the lighting circumstances, you may ensure that your photos accurately depict the scene's actual hues. By doing this, you can prevent fluorescent lighting from adding undesirable tints or color casts to your photos.

Incandescent

The color temperature of most light bulbs is too warm, although this is compensated for by the INCANDESCENT white balance option. If you wanted to use the Joe McNally method, which involves using an orange CTO gel on the flash and the INCANDESCENT white balance setting, you would also use this option. As a result, the whole image appears gloomy, depressing, and blue. The WB, on the other hand, will remove the orange light from the flash and give the subjects a normal appearance.

Underwater

This one is really simple. It lessens the deep waters' vibrant blue hue. Since I don't often take Fuji photos underwater, I haven't utilized it. However, you should utilize this white balance if you own an aquatic property.

How to Adjust White Balance

A fine-tuning slider appears when you press MENU/OK after choosing a white balance setting. Use the focus stick, also known as the focus lever, to adjust the white balance.

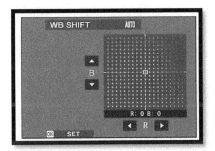

After selecting a white balance option, press DISP/BACK to close the menu without making any changes. While adjusting the white balance ring, the focus stick cannot be pushed over a line.

Personalized White Balance

To adjust white balance for certain lighting conditions, choose $\square_1$, $\square_2$, or $\square_3$ and refer to a white item. Colored materials may also be used to add color to images. Press the shutter button all the way down to measure white balance after a white balance target appears. You can either press MENU/OK to select the most recent value and display the fine-tuning dialog or press DISP/BACK to select the most recent custom value and exit without measuring white balance.

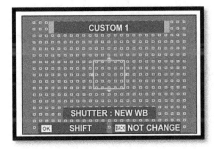

❖ To adjust the white balance to the measured value, choose MENU/OK if "COMPLETED!" is shown.

❖ If "UNDER" appears, try raising the exposure setting.

❖ Try again with a lower exposure adjustment if "OVER" is shown.

About Color Temperature

Adjust the white balance to match the light source's color temperature. It is possible to alter the color temperature to make images "warmer" or "colder," or to create colors that are quite different from those seen in the actual world. From the white balance option, choose K. The presently chosen color temperature will be shown.

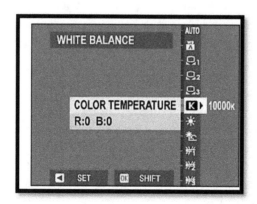

Press MENU/OK after adjusting the color temperature with the focus stick (focus lever). There will be a fine-tuning dialog available.

❖ To change the color temperature in 10K steps, use the command dial on the back.

❖ Select values between 2500 and 10,000 K.

❖ After selecting a color temperature, press DISP/BACK to quit without adjusting the white balance.

To draw attention to a certain degree of fine-tuning, use the focus stick. To make the changes take effect, press MENU/OK. The display will show the color temperature you choose.

What is Color Temperature?

The objective measurement of a light source's color, given in Kelvin (K), is called color temperature. Higher color temperature light sources are tinted blue, lower color temperature light sources are yellow or red, and light sources with a color temperature equal to that of direct sunshine seem white.

D RANGE PRIORITY

By preventing information loss in highlights and shadows, particularly in high contrast environments, this feature aims to produce photos that seem more realistic.

- ❖ **AUTO:** For the best dynamic range, the contrast is automatically adjusted dependent on the illumination.
- ❖ **STRONG:** Provides vibrant highlights and shadows by enhancing dynamic range for high contrast images.
- ❖ Moderate shift to dynamic range is a weakness. This works best in situations with a moderate amount of contrast that need some adjustment but not as much as ones with a lot of contrast.
- ❖ **OFF:** Disables contrast reduction, preserving the dynamic range of the picture while preserving its original contrast levels.

By choosing the appropriate D RANGE PRIORITY setting based on the scene's contrast levels, photographers may effectively preserve information in both the bright and dark portions of a picture, producing more balanced and aesthetically beautiful image graphs.

- ❖ While WEAK is accessible from ISO 250 to 12800, STRONG is available from ISO 500 to 12800.
- ❖ The TONE CURVE and DYNAMIC RANGE will be automatically adjusted if you choose an option other than OFF. Select OFF if you want to change these parameters by hand.

The tone curve

Highlights and shadows may be either sharper or softer based on the tone curve. To make highlights and shadows more intense, use a greater value. To make them softer, decrease the number.

You already know how beautiful the X Series JPEGs seem as soon as they are taken, don't you? We all like this feature of Fuji cameras. To ensure that you obtain a fantastic picture with vibrant colors and loads of dynamic depth, you may choose the proper Film Simulation, change the exposure, and examine the LCD screen. It is okay to shoot JPEG in a variety of lighting circumstances since the camera's image processor manages most parameters so well. But what happens if you're filming in awful lighting? You could shoot RAW images. Although Fuji RAW files include a lot of information, shooting RAW requires you to spend time post-processing your images when you weren't at your best at the time.

The ability to choose a kind of film, take the picture, and be done is helpful, even if it's not a bad thing. If only there was a method to handle dim lighting while using JPEG format for photography. Thankfully, there is. The HIGHLIGHT TONE and SHADOW TONE settings (also called H TONE and S TONE) in the Q menu are quite helpful, even though many Fuji photographers I speak with have never used them. You can adjust the brightness of the lights and darks with HIGHLIGHT TONE and SHADOW TONE, much as if the camera had post-processing features built right in. On the other hand, the command dial lets you control them rather without using knobs. This lets you make changes to the picture before you take it instead of after. The LCD may be used to see the results. With "+" adding and "-" subtracting, you may adjust the contrast from +4 to -2 with these values. This makes it easy to adjust your really bright tones and make the blacks darker or brighter.

Highlight Tone

Highlights are hard to execute. Your photos shouldn't have a lot of blown highlights or shadows. Most of us use the highlights as the basis for our exposure calculations. You can't get them back after you blast them out and send them flying off the right side of the histogram. The same is true with shadows, albeit most of them don't bother us. The photographer's best buddy is shadow.

You may employ shadows to create striking forms and visual intrigue in your photos. But we seldom benefit from blown highlights. We put a lot of effort into reducing or eliminating areas of the sky or water that seem too bright in photos. You may darken any areas of your picture that are excessively bright by using the HIGHLIGHT TONE slider. Blonded-out highlights cannot be fully fixed, although they may be made less visible by reducing their strength. Because of this, the HIGHLIGHT TONE setting is probably less helpful than the SHADOW TONE control, but if you're shooting high-contrast JPEGs, it may still be a fine and practical choice.

HIGHLIGHT TONE SET TO 0

HIGHLIGHT TONE set to -2

About Shadow Tone

The SHADOW TONE control may be used in many different ways. As mentioned earlier, I often utilize this parameter to tweak color levels and fine-tune the film simulation I've selected. Additionally, I'll utilize it to adjust contrast and highlight darker tones. It's excellent for this. For instance, let's imagine you want to include more black people to enhance the drama and contrast. To make your shadows darker, move the "+" button on SHADOW TONE to the right. What if you want to give the shadows more depth and complexity but already have a picture with a lot of contrast? To make the picture wider, move the slider back to -2.

COLOR

With the exception of the ability to adjust the value from -4 to +4, the COLOR control functions similarly to the HIGHLIGHT TONE and SHADOW TONE controls. On the "plus" side, changes enhance color intensity and contrast. Modifications push them to the "minus" side. Compared to what you get when you set the SHADOW TONE to 4, these effects are far better. Your audience won't notice anything you do here, and nothing you do will stand out. Once again, this will just alter the appearance of your JPEGs. It will only affect the JPEG screen on the rear of the camera, not how your RAW files look.

When Is This Control Useful?

The best way to answer that question, in my opinion, is to say that it is totally up to you. This setting, in my opinion, is more about giving you more creative possibilities than it is about adjusting your exposure. This impact might be really helpful as long as it doesn't provide a wide picture. It has made the process of "color grading" my film simulations easier. I sometimes increase a scene's brightness to make it more noticeable, but I also use it to soften the colors and create a more subdued palette. You may enhance the color of your VELVIA picture or soften the CLASSIC CHROME or PRO Neg photos. Your reds are too intense and are overpowering the histogram, even if you may truly want the VELVIA effect. To return them to a more realistic range, you may utilize this control. The allure of the X-M5 is that it produces excellent photographs straight out of the box, yet these adjustments are readily adjustable on a computer. Additional built-in options let you adjust and produce the precise look you want depending on your topic, your inspiration, and your current mood.

SHARPNESS

SHARPNESS, the last option in this set, allows you to choose the overall sharpness of your JPEGs. The range is +4 to -4. You may adjust how tight and crisp the photographs seem with this option, even though your Fuji image processor will sharpen the file automatically. Like the other three options (COLOR, SHADOW TONE, and HIGHLIGHT TONE), this is probably going to stay mostly unaltered. You know where to go if you ever need to give your photos more contrast, softness, or roughness. When taking pictures with poor contrast, think about using a softer preset. Turn this setting up a little, or a lot! Again, it all comes down to choice when it comes to action, street, and other themes that could call for a bit more edge. What style do you want for your pictures? There is no right response or setting. Technical issues that would cause a lot of negative comments in certain camera groups may sometimes be found among the world's most beautiful photographs. If you capture a captivating subject in great light at the right time, it doesn't matter if you make a few little adjustments to the image's color, sharpness, or tones. As long as you are happy with the results, everything is fine. The fact is that almost all of the exceptional images have undergone some kind of alteration. Changes to the HIGHLIGHT TONE, SHADOW TONE, COLOR, and SHARPNESS settings may be saved using the EDIT/preserve CUSTOM SETTING menu option.

HIGH ISO NR

The purpose of this feature is to reduce noise in images captured at high ISO settings, particularly in low light conditions.

❖ Higher values provide cleaner and more aesthetically pleasing images by smoothing curves and lowering noise. Even though clarity may be compromised, this level is advised when noise suppression is crucial.

- ❖ Lower values reduce noise and preserve picture borders. If photographers want to maintain crisp, clear images even in low light, they should choose this option.

By adjusting the HIGH ISO NR level to their shooting parameters and personal preferences, photographers may achieve the greatest possible balance between picture sharpness and noise reduction, resulting in high-quality photographs under a variety of lighting circumstances.

CLARITY

With the help of this effective tool, you can make photos sharper and more readable while maintaining the most consistent tones in the highlights and shadows.

- ❖ Increasing the CLARITY option improves the definition and clarity of images. This enhances overall clarity and helps things stand out. Photographs that need a bold and dramatic look, like landscape or architectural shots, are best suited for higher values.
- ❖ The effect is lessened and clarity is decreased when lower CLARITY levels are used. This might give the color a softer, more airy appearance, which is great for pictures or situations that call for a softer, more dreamy appearance.

By adjusting the CLARITY option to suit each image's requirements, photographers may get the required impact while maintaining the image's natural appearance and tone balance.

Long Exposure NR

Select ON if you want to lessen mottling caused by prolonged exposures. There will be less mottling with longer exposures at this level. By covertly taking a second exposure with the shutter closed, it achieves its objective. By comparing the two frames, the noise in the second frame is then removed from the original image. By doing this, the exposure's noise level is decreased. Therefore, turning on this option almost always improves picture quality. Occasionally, there is a significant disparity. When the shutter is released, this makes the camera process your picture twice as slowly. Because it relies on your camera and aperture settings, it is not always appropriate for extended exposure durations. LONG EXPOSURE NR seems to work best with exposures of one minute or more, although it also seems to work with shorter exposures at narrower apertures, such f/16. But no one knows for sure. The only people who know what is happening are Fuji's experts, and they are remaining silent. Reiterating everything, using this option will result in twice as many long-exposure photos, but they will look far better. Bring a book or a drink to pass the time while taking long exposure photos if you don't want to wait.

LENS MODULATION OPTIMIZER

To enhance definition by compensating for diffraction and a little loss of focus at the edge of the lens, choose ON.

COLOR SPACE

In photography, a color space is the spectrum of colors that may be produced with a certain piece of gear or medium. In a variety of media, including electronic devices, color is shown differently. To make it possible for cameras, computers, displays, and different kinds of paper to match colors more precisely, a set of standard color spaces was developed. For digital images, you may choose either Adobe RGB or sRGB as your color space. Adobe RGB is the industry standard for corporate printing, however sRGB is used by the majority of devices.

❖ When displaying photos on displays, TVs, and the internet, use sRGB. A color space called sRGB ensures that colors show up uniformly on all devices and platforms.

❖ Adobe RGB is appropriate for commercial applications and professional printing because it offers a greater color gamut than sRGB. It performs best with high-quality photos or in situations where color accuracy is essential, like print or graphic design.

Despite having a wider color gamut than sRGB, not all devices and monitors can display all of Adobe RGB's colors. This implies that an Adobe RGB picture you upload online may not seem to have the same colors in real life as it does in the app. Your shared photos will be exactly like the originals if you take them in the sRGB color space. However, some of the color vibrancy of your photos may be lost when you print them. Which color scheme is best? The short answer is that if you're mainly taking pictures for the web and displaying them on digital devices, you should shoot in sRGB. For the vast majority of circumstances, this is the most suitable setting. You should always convert your photos to sRGB before posting them online if you are a professional photographer or often print your work. This will give your photos the greatest color information. When playing back RAW files, utilize the RAW edit option to perform this modification. You may make sure that your photos are appropriate for their intended usage, whether it is professional printing or digital display, by selecting the appropriate COLOR SPACE. Additionally, you can ensure that the colors are accurate and constant across all media.

Pixel mapping

This software may assist you in correcting any bright spots or other issues in your photos or videos.

To choose this choice:

❖ Press MENU/OK on the shooting display to bring up the settings menu.
❖ Select the tab for Image Quality Setting.
❖ Choose PIXEL MAPPING and MENU/OK to begin the pixel mapping procedure.

This feature helps identify and fix any damaged pixels on your camera sensor, guaranteeing that your high-quality images and videos are free of undesired artifacts and irregularities.

Keep in mind the following while using your camera for pixel mapping:

❖ **No assurance:** Pixel mapping may provide surprising outcomes. It could help with bright spot issues, but it might not get rid of every odd element in your picture or video.

❖ **Battery Level:** Make sure your camera's battery is completely charged before doing any pixel mapping. The process can halt if the battery is not completely charged.

❖ **Take Temperature into Account:** Pixel mapping may not function correctly if it overheats. Perform this task in a more tranquil environment to prevent problems.

❖ **Processing time:** It may take many tens of seconds to map pixels. To get the best results, wait patiently and allow the camera enough time to make the necessary changes.

Select Custom Setting

You may retrieve settings from custom settings banks 1–7 (CUSTOM 1–CUSTOM 7) by using EDIT/SAVE CUSTOM SETTING.

Banks			
[NOTHING SELECTED]	[CUSTOM 1]	[CUSTOM 2]	[CUSTOM 3]
[CUSTOM 4]	[CUSTOM 5]	[CUSTOM 6]	[CUSTOM 7]

The settings you choose before shutting the camera off will remain in place when you turn it on again. (However, the self-timer will always return to OFF.) BASE will be the name of the custom configuration you choose or are using. It will appear as BASE plus your C settings number on certain cameras, as BASE/C1. Keep in mind that any modifications you make to your BASE setting will not impact the default banks, if you haven't altered them, or the custom bank you have selected. Assume that the VELVIA option is kept unchecked and that you are shooting in C2. Your current bank will be referred to as BASE/C2, or just BASE, if you set the SHADOW TONE to +3. The camera will revert to BASE/C2 mode with the VELVIA and SHADOW TONE +3 settings if you switch it off and back on. You will go back to C1 and continue ascending the hills if you scroll away from BASE. When you arrive, it will still be VELVIA as that was your default selection for C2. The shadow tone, however, will be set to 0. You will ultimately return to BASE, sometimes referred to as BASE/C2, if you keep traveling. The same will apply to ST+3 and VELVIA. This implies that until you make another adjustment, whatever modifications you make to the IMAGE QUALITY settings will stay in force. Consider BASE to be your current environment.

Edit/Save Custom Configuration

What happens if you choose to modify any of your custom settings? By selecting the EDIT/SAVE CUSTOM SETTING menu item, you may do this and create your own unique banks for C1-7. To modify any of the C1-7 banks while in shooting mode, press MENU/OK to bring up the shooting menu. Scroll down to the IMAGE QUALITY SETTING tab, choose EDIT/SAVE CUSTOM SETTING, and then click MENU/OK to complete the process. After that, choose one of the seven banks and either click OK once more or scroll to the right. By clicking on them or selecting OK, you may now modify any of the following settings by changing the values as necessary.

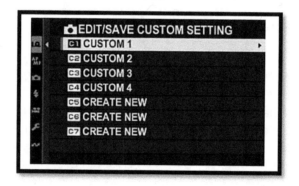

Click "OK" after you've finished each modification. Next, go back and update the next one, and so on. Select SAVE CURRENT SETTINGS from the menu at the top if you want to keep the picture quality settings you've previously changed. All of your current camera settings will remain in that bank as a result. In any event, use the BACK button and then OK to be sure you saved your work. After choosing OK and hitting BACK, be sure to press the OK button.

Changing Custom Preferences

Modify the present custom settings banks

❖ Select MENU/OK after navigating to the shooting menu. Next, choose EDIT/SAVE CUSTOM SETTINGS > IMAGE QUALITY SETTINGS.

➤ To save the recording settings for a movie, choose MOVIE SETTING from the movie menu, followed by EDIT/SAVE CUSTOM SETTING.

❖ Click MENU/OK after choosing the custom settings bank.

❖ Click OK or MENU after you have chosen EDIT/CHECK.

❖ A list of shooting menu choices will appear on the camera; choose the one you want to change and hit MENU/OK. As necessary, swap out the chosen item.

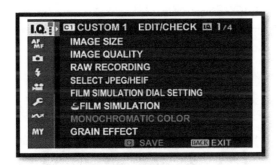

❖ Click MENU/OK to save your modifications and go back to the shooting menu list. Make any other changes you like. The modifications made to the picture or video menus will be indicated with red dots if DISABLE is selected under IMAGE QUALITY SETTING > AUTO UPDATE CUSTOM SETTING or video SETTING > AUTO UPDATE CUSTOM SETTING. Changes won't be instantly stored, however.

➤ Click Q after selecting the items to save changes to the list.

➤ Go back to Step 3 and choose SAVE THE CHANGES to have your changes take effect. To reverse any modifications and return to the initial configuration, choose RESET THE CHANGES.

➤ Nothing will change if you copy an item with a red dot.

Copying Custom Configurations

Custom settings are erased in the second bank when you switch them between them. The destination bank will have a replica of the source bank's name if it changes.

❖ Select MENU/OK after navigating to the shooting menu. Next, choose EDIT/SAVE CUSTOM SETTINGS > IMAGE QUALITY SETTINGS.

> Go to the movie menu; choose MOVIE SETTING, and then EDIT/SAVE CUSTOM SETTING to save the recording settings.
❖ Click MENU/OK after the source bank has been chosen.
❖ Choose "COPY" and then press "OK" or "MENU."
❖ Click MENU/OK after selecting the bank (C1–C7). A confirmation dial box will appear.
> Any modifications made to the custom settings of the target bank will be lost.
❖ Choose MENU/OK after clicking OK.
> Any preexisting settings will be replaced by the supplied settings when they are moved to the target bank.

Eliminating Custom Configurations

Some custom settings banks include settings that may be deleted.
❖ Select MENU/OK after navigating to the shooting menu. Next, choose EDIT/SAVE CUSTOM SETTINGS > IMAGE QUALITY SETTINGS.
> Go to the movie menu; choose MOVIE SETTING, and then EDIT/SAVE CUSTOM SETTING to save the recording settings.
❖ Click MENU/OK after you've chosen your favorite custom settings bank.
❖ A confirmation dial box will appear. Next, choose "ERASE" and hit "OK" or "MENU."
❖ Choose MENU/OK after clicking OK. You will lose any personalized settings that were stored in the selected bank.

Changing the names of Custom Settings Banks

Change some custom settings banks

❖ Select MENU/OK after navigating to the shooting menu. Next, choose EDIT/SAVE CUSTOM SETTINGS > IMAGE QUALITY SETTINGS.
> Select MOVIE SETTING and then EDIT/SAVE CUSTOM SETTING to save the movie recording settings.
❖ Click MENU/OK after you've chosen your favorite custom settings bank.
❖ Click OK or MENU after selecting EDIT CUSTOM NAME.
❖ Press SET after giving the custom settings bank a new name. A new name will be given to the selected bank.

AUTOMATIC CUSTOM SETTING UPDATE

You may choose whether stored modifications to custom settings are applied right away.

- ❖ **ENABLE:** Changes made to banks CUSTOM 1–7's custom settings are immediately updated.
- ❖ **DISABLE:** Modifications won't take effect right away. Custom parameters may only be changed manually.

ADAPTOR MOUNT SETTING

For lenses that are attached to a mount adapter, change the parameters. Multiple lens settings (LENS 1-6) may be saved by the camera. D IS TORTION, COLOR SHADING, and PEripHERAL ILLUMINATION may all be corrected using lenses that are attached to a M mount adaptor. The movie mod is likewise impacted by any modifications made to this item.

SETTING FOR THE FOCAL LENGTH

Now let's talk about the focal length of the lens.

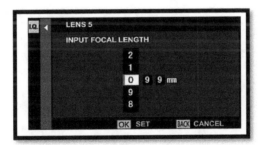

Correction of Distortion

To adjust for PINCUSHION or BARREL distortion, choose STRONG, MEDIUM, or WEAK.

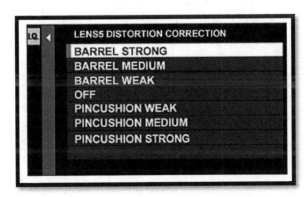

Correction of Color Shading

Each corner's color (shading) differences from the frame's center and edges may be altered independently. Use the procedures listed below to apply color shading correction.

❖ Select a corner by using the rear command dial. A triangle is used to symbolize the selected corner.

❖ Use the focus stick (lever) to adjust the shade until the chosen corner and the image's center are the same color.

➢ Press the focus stick to the left or right to alter the colors on the cyan-red axis.

➢ You can press the focus stick up or down to adjust the colors on the blue-yellow axis.

To determine how much color shading correction is needed, try taking a picture of a gray piece of paper or a blue sky.

CORRECTION OF PERIPHERAL ILLUMINATION

Select a number between -5 and +5. Selecting negative values decreases peripheral illumination, whereas selecting positive values increases it. Negative values provide the appearance of images captured with a pinhole camera or an old lens, whereas positive values are preferred for antique lenses.

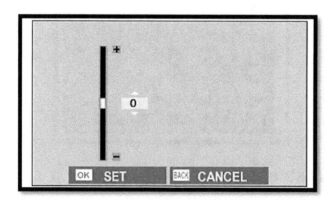

To find out how much is needed, take pictures of the blue sky or a piece of gray paper while adjusting the peripheral illumination setting.

CHAPTER SEVEN

COMPREHENDING MANUAL AND AUTOFOCUS

AF/MF Settings - Focus Menus

Fujifilm cameras use a novel hybrid focusing technique that combines strong, state-of-the-art algorithms with contrast and phase recognition sensors. The end product is a fast, precise, and very effective focus gadget. You can even use the back button to concentrate on them. Nearly every Fuji camera has the ability to track moving objects, latch on a subject quickly, and shoot at high frame rates in fast motion. Additionally, they feature excellent Face Detection technology that lets you shoot pictures of individuals without shifting focus. From the MENU/OK button on the picture shooting display, choose the AF/MF SETTING tab to see the AF/MF settings.

The Options Available

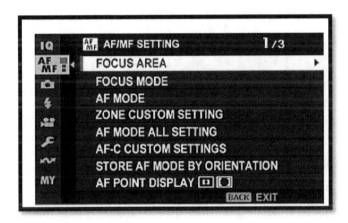

- ❖ FOCUS AREA
- ❖ FOCUS MODE
- ❖ AF MODE
- ❖ ZONE CUSTOM SETTING
- ❖ AF MODE ALL SETTING
- ❖ AF-C CUSTOM SETTINGS
- ❖ STORE AF MODE BY ORIENTATION
- ❖ AF POINT DISPLAY
- ❖ WRAP FOCUS POINT
- ❖ NUMBER OF FOCUS POINTS
- ❖ PRE-AF
- ❖ AF ILLUMINATOR
- ❖ FACE/EYE DETECTION SETTING
- ❖ SUBJECT DETECTION SETTING

- ❖ AF+MF
- ❖ MF ASSIST
- ❖ INTERLOCK MF ASSIST & FOCUS RING
- ❖ FOCUS CHECK
- ❖ INTERLOCK SPOT AE & FOCUS AREA
- ❖ INSTANT AF SETTING
- ❖ DEPTH-OF-FIELD SCALE
- ❖ RELEASE/FOCUS PRIORITY
- ❖ AF RANGE LIMITER
- ❖ TOUCH SCREEN MODE

FOCUS AREA

You may choose your FOCUS AREA from this menu item, but you should never use it for that purpose. By default, the FOCUS AREA is selected by pressing the button on the bottom thumb pad. This method just requires a single push to get there. You will still need to hit two keys even if you have FOCUS AREA at the top of your MY MENU. Use focus as soon as possible since you will probably need to respond swiftly.

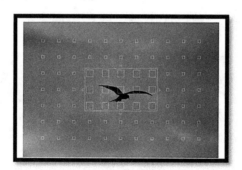

AF MODE

With the help of the four settings—SINGLE AF, ZONE AF, WIDE/TRACKING, and ALL— you can frame and track your subject with remarkable ease, speed, and accuracy. (All three modes are not available on the original X Series cameras.) The AF ALL facilitates seamless transitions between all three settings. To choose or reposition your focus points, activate FOCUS AREA. Use the "down" button on the thumb pad or the AF joystick to move the green AF box. You may either use the joystick or touch the relevant part of the screen to choose your focus location.

A single AF

Selecting one of the AF locations shown on the LCD is all that is required when using SINGLE AF. Selecting a focus point on the rear of the camera may help achieve this. Either AF-S or AF-C may be used with SINGLE AF mode. While AF-C is used to follow moving things that remain in the same spot in the frame, including those immediately in front of or behind you, AF-S is used to capture stationary subjects. Adjust the rear command dial to the appropriate size and place the AF box above the subject for SINGLE AF with still subjects. Previous versions only let you to utilize the 3x5 region in the center of the frame for your focus grid while shooting SINGLE AF in AF-C mode on Continuous High. This corresponds to the 15-phase Detect AF spots on the sensor. About 40% of the frame is made up of a Phase Detect grid with 169 points in a 13x13 arrangement in the most recent versions. You may put a focus point anywhere in the picture, even in the corners, which is the brilliance of SINGLE AF. Fuji cameras allow you to focus anywhere, unlike standard DSLR cameras that only let you focus in the middle of the picture. How you arrange your photos is entirely up to you. To change the size of the specified area, use the command dial on the back. Use the AF joystick or the directional thumb tab buttons to adjust its position in the frame. Only if the little green focus box shows up on the LCD will this be feasible. I use the SINGLE AF option when I need to be really accurate and make sure the camera is focused on the right target. One instance is when you are able to concentrate on a little element in the frame or a topic that blends in with the background of the picture. I may utilize SINGLE AF in AF-C mode if I'm sure my subject won't move around too much in the frame. However, I usually utilize AF-S mode while using SINGLE AF.

Zone AF

ZONE AF makes use of several AF points. Rather, you use a set of points. To match the size and placement of your topic in the frame, you may alter the group's dimensions. Once your focus zone has been established, drag the whole grid across the frame using the focus point selection tool. The camera will choose one or more AF points to focus on your subject when you utilize ZONE AF, even if it is moving away. Both AF-S and AF-C modes are supported. those that are still or moving slowly should use the AF-S mode; those that move quickly should use the AF-C mode. My favorite setup is ZONE AF, which works with both AF-S and AF-C modes. In AF-C mode, I'll utilize ZONE AF to follow any motion or subjects moving fast across the frame, and in AF-S mode, I'll use it to concentrate on things that aren't moving quickly or at all and are hard to locate with SINGLE AF. Golden retrievers, motorcyclists, runners, motorbikes, skiers, and athletic kids and grandkids will all love this place for shooting birds. To be prepared to photograph anything, I make sure my AF-C cameras are in ZONE AF mode when I switch them on. Since you don't have to be as precise when selecting your focus point initially, ZONE AF is the most adaptable AF option. Additionally, it will keep track of subjects as they travel between the frame's several AF sites. As with SINGLE AF, your zone is restricted to the Phase Detect pixel grid in the middle of your LCD when shooting in Continuous High mode. I determine the size of my zone for ZONE AF by looking at my subject's position in the frame, its likelihood of moving across the frame, its size, and whether there are any other objects in the frame that could unintentionally divert the focus of a large zone.

Wide/tracking AF

In this setup, the AF system is in Full Auto mode. It's perfect for photographing challenging environments, a variety of moving objects, or uncertain subject matter. If you're unsure of which focus point to use or just want to shoot without thinking about AF, WIDE/TRACKING is usually the best option. Both AF-S and AF-C modes are supported. The camera instantly transitions to WIDE/TRACKING mode when you flick the switch in Full Auto mode. If there are people in the frame, objects aren't moving too fast or erratically, or my subject is cleared, unobstructed, and out of the way of anything that may interfere with the focus system, I select this choice when I'm certain the camera can focus. I can hire someone else to do my focus job if I need to, and I sometimes desire to do so.

AF All

All you need to do in this mode is effortlessly navigate between your AF points' various forms and the three basic focus modes. Rotate the rear command dial to change the size of a green focus box that is chosen in AF ALL mode. The camera will automatically switch to the next AF setting when the current one reaches its limit. It will return to SINGLE AF with the smallest point as soon as you hit WIDE or TRACK. When you have a variety of themes, sizes, and movements, this works very well. If the subject moves or takes up more area in the frame when using SINGLE AF, you may swap modes without using the Fn button. Just keep turning the command dial on the rear. Switching between modes only requires two or three Fn button pushes, even though AF ALL speeds up your photography and smoothes the transition.

ZONE CUSTOM SETTING

Make your own focus zones to be used when AF MODE is set for ZONE.

AF MODE ALL SETTINGS

When AF MODE is set to ALL, choose the area of focus that will be utilized. The focal area and shooting manner are up to you to decide. When the focus mode is S (AF-S) or C (AF-C), you may adjust this.

CUSTOM AF-C SETTINGS

In focus mode C, choose the choices for following the focus. While Set 6 provides more customizable focus-tracking settings, Sets 1–5 are subject-specific.

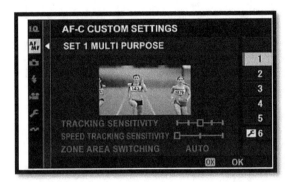

SET 1: Multipurpose

By default, the AF-C is set to MULTI PURPOSE, with AUTO for Zone Area Switching, zero for Speed Tracking, and medium for Tracking Sensitivity. When your subjects move at a consistent pace, this works well for a variety of movements. As demonstrated in the picture below, this might be used to capture races, animals that move steadily, or topics that are likely to vanish for a little period of time. I experimented with this setting for a long when I initially bought the camera to learn how it operated. It cannot properly handle certain kinds of activity. Try adjusting to a different setting if you're unable to remain focused or follow topics.

Set 2: Ignore the Obstacle

When your subjects are moving behind trees or other obstacles that block your view, or when they are momentarily escaping the frame or the focus zone you have selected, this option is ideal.

It will take a bit longer to get to a new zone if you increase the tracking sensitivity. The emphasis will stay in the middle of the zone when Zone Area Switching is set to middle. It won't hold onto anything at the boundary of the zone. This mode is what I usually utilize when I can't concentrate on my topic. For the themes I often photograph, I guess this is one of my two favorite websites. It does not go off topic too soon and maintains concentration on the current topic. This allows you to be pretty creative and adaptable in terms of maintaining focus on your primary topic, even if it is contending for frame space or piercing through something you would want to remain out of focus. My sharp topic should usually be placed far back in the frame, behind other objects. You can keep your lock in place while doing this with this option.

Examples include photographing animals in a bustling desert, concentrating on people in a crowd, capturing movement in a dense woodland, or a motorcycle approaching another racer (see picture above). Similar to a cheetah.

SET 3: Subject Acceleration/Deceleration

This mode, with Speed Tracking Sensitivity set to 2, is best for photographing subjects with sudden movements and significant speed variations. Using methods intended to handle non-smooth motion; the point of focus will stay in the image's foreground, closest to the camera. It's thus excellent for photographing animals and sports where the subject's pace is always changing. I don't typically utilize this option. It's still a helpful option for photographing certain things, but I haven't found the perfect topics to try it on yet. According to Fuji, their LM lenses with Linear AF Motor—the 90mm, 50-140mm, 100-400mm, 16-55mm, 55-200mm, 18-55mm, and 18-135mm—are most affected by this setting when used for high-speed tracking.

Set 4: Unexpectedly Showing Subject

Another AF-C Custom Setting that I really like is this one. The camera is ready to focus immediately on the topic that enters the frame when setting Tracking Sensitivity is set to the lowest setting and Zone Area Switching is set to FRONT. The camera can swiftly transition to the correct zone since the tracking sensitivity is low and the nearest item in the picture is the focus. This option is quite useful and efficient for a variety of action, sports, and animal photos. It enables you to swiftly capture subjects as they appear in the shot after setting up the desired scene. Choose the AF Zone closest to where you expect the subject to enter the frame for the greatest results. Try this mode if you're having trouble getting and keeping a decent lock on your subject matter and it's not a "obstacle."

SET 5: Subject Moving Erratically

By increasing the Tracking Sensitivity, you can maintain the camera's focus on your target. The AF system employs predictive methods that are most appropriate for individuals with irregular movements when the Speed Tracking Sensitivity is set to 2. Zone Area Switching is set to AUTO in this instance, so even if the subject moves in and out of the focus zone or is not directly in front of the camera, the lock will remain in place. For shooting sports like football, lacrosse, and soccer, where directions and speeds often change, this is unquestionably the greatest choice. It works well with kids, grandchildren, and pets as well. Photographers who like capturing fast-moving, flitting birds and other animals that move in a "skittish" or hyperactive manner will love this location.

Set 6: Custom-made

In the CUSTOM bank, you may manually alter one or three AF settings and save the outcome as a custom preset. In other words, you may adjust your AF-C Custom Settings to be ideal for the kind of movement your subject exhibits and then be prepared to ring whenever you choose. You could want to document a sport or topic that is overcoming certain obstacles. To ensure that it stays in focus for a longer period of time, you may wish to increase the tracking sensitivity. You may want the camera to record topics faster if you're recording a variety of actions. It is possible to lower the tracking sensitivity. What about issues that emerge suddenly and move in peculiar ways? Zone Area Switching may be set to AUTO, and Speed Tracking Sensitivity can be adjusted to 2. It's possible that you are photographing the same topic again and over. You may adjust the parameters until they suit you best, and then store them for subsequent use. In any event, the AF -C CUSTOM SETTINGS menu is a very helpful feature that might help you improve the operation of your camera and customize it to fit your unique shooting preferences.

FOCUS TRACKING OPTIONS

Below is an explanation of certain parameters from a focus tracking dataset.

TRACKING SENSITIVITY

If the subject is gone for a brief moment, the camera will move to a new AF zone according to the TRACKING SENSITIVITY setting. For instance, the subject may momentarily leave the frame, vanish behind a tree, or be in front of something else. The camera will immediately move to a new place in an attempt to catch the subject again if the setting is set to 0. The system will remain stuck in the current zone for progressively longer periods of time between settings 1 and 4.

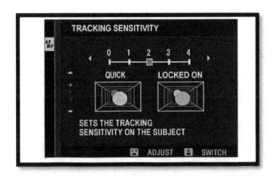

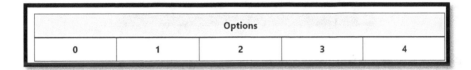

If the topic is moving swiftly across the screen, you may choose setting 0; if it disappears behind something else and you know it will emerge soon, you can choose one of the higher settings.

SPEED TRACKING SENSITIVITY

Depending on whether the subject is moving at a constant or variable speed, you may choose how the camera follows it using SPEED TRACKING SENSITIVITY. The minuscule lag between focusing the subject and triggering the shutter must also be taken into consideration by the camera. Setting 0 should be used by subjects traveling steadily, whereas option 2 should be used by those moving more erratically or who are accelerating or decelerating. Setting 1 provides topics traveling at varying speeds with a fair balance. While setting 2 could be suitable for shooting youngsters or sports like soccer, setting 0 might be perfect for shooting road bikes and soaring birds.

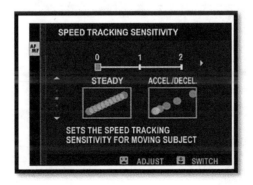

Zone Areas Switching

You may decide which area of your chosen focus zone should be given priority by utilizing ZONE part SWITCHING, which is only possible if you're using ZONE AF.

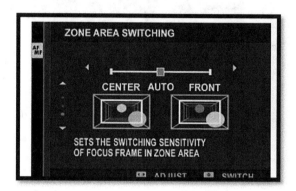

Middle keeps your attention at the zone's center. FRONT tells the camera to concentrate on the surrounding area when your main subject leaves the frame. AUTO keeps up with the topic—or portion of the topic—that you first concentrated on. When photographing a moving subject that quickly vanishes behind another object in the frame, such as a biker or an animal hiding behind a tree, CENTER is a terrific method to keep track of them. When a person enters the frame rapidly or you are unsure of their direction, you should employ FRONT. The AUTO mode is the default for a lot of topics and tasks.

Set the values

Below are the parameter values for each set.

AF-C CUSTOM SETTINGS	TRACKING SENSITIVITY	SPEED TRACKING SENSITIVITY	ZONE AREA SWITCHING
SET 1	2	0	AUTO
SET 2	3	0	CENTER
SET 3	2	2	AUTO
SET 4	0	1	FRONT
SET 5	3	2	AUTO

Options for Custom Focus Tracking

Use the procedures below to modify the parameters in Set 6.
 ❖ Choose SET 6 CUSTOM under AF-C Custom Settings.

❖ To highlight objects and make adjustments, use the focus stick (lever) and the front command dial. Press the Drive Button to restore the settings to their initial settings.

❖ Press DISP/BACK once the adjustments are complete.

STORE THE AF MODE BY ORIENTATION

By just glancing at the screen, many of the camera's menu items can determine whether you're holding it vertically or horizontally. One of my favorite focus menu options is this one. It is one of the most helpful options in the whole focus menu and was included in a recent software upgrade. The placements of AF MODE and AF AREA are the identical whether shooting vertically or horizontally in off mode. Put your AF point in the top right corner of the picture, assuming you're shooting horizontally. The same spot will be recorded when the camera is moved up and down, but it will now be seen in the upper left corner of the picture. You would have to relocate your focus point across the frame every time the camera moved if you were shooting and attempting to concentrate on a subject on the right side of the frame while alternating between horizontal and vertical pictures.

Naturally, it takes time to change the AF point. It may be annoying to constantly move the focus points when you rotate the camera while photographing a moving subject or alternating between horizontal and vertical positions. This tool is crucial because of this. The camera will remember where you put the focus point and maintain it independently for each direction if you choose FOCUS AREA ONLY from the menu. When you rotate the camera, you will only need to enter the new position of the AF point once. You won't have to choose your AF point again since the camera will remember it when you switch it back on. Selecting this option allows you to set a different frame portion and focus mode for both horizontal and vertical framing since the camera will remember both your focus area and your AF MODE. For horizontal pieces, you may use SINGLE POINT AF; for verticals, you can use ZONE or WIDE/TRACKING.

To have the most control, I always have this on. Having to switch it off while filming is unthinkable. The fact that they added this option, which I often use, made me extremely pleased. It's an excellent tool for taking pictures, sports, action, or any topic that requires rapid transitions between horizontal and vertical perspectives.

The AF Point Display

When in AF ZONE or WIDE/TRACKING focus mode, this option shows the various focus frames on the LCD. It is simple to identify the focus frames since they appear as a see-through grid on the LCD. You may see your AF zone's precise dimensions and point locations, which might help you arrange your shots. If you would rather have a bright, clear LCD without grids or guidelines, you may wish to turn it off even if it isn't in the way. However, the grid may be helpful if you're new to the X series, particularly when capturing moving objects or zones of different sizes.

WRAP FOCUS POINT

Choose whether the focus area selection is limited by the display's borders or "wraps around" from one end to the other.
- ❖ **Activated:** The focus-area feature "wraps around" the corners of the screen. Stated differently, if you go to the edge of the screen while switching focus regions, the pick will start again from the other edge, creating a loop.
- ❖ **DISABLE:** Turning off this setting limits the focus area selection to the boundaries of the display. That is, once you approach the edge of the display and switch focus regions, you cannot continue scrolling in the same manner.

Turning this feature on or off may affect how fast and easy it is to adjust focus zones, depending on your shooting preferences and style. If you regularly transition between focus areas and hate coming back from the edge of the display, you may find that turning on focus-area wrapping saves you time. If you want more precise control over the focus area selection and don't want to inadvertently scroll beyond the display boundaries, you could wish to remove this option.

FOCUS POINT NUMBER

Select how many focus points can be used to select a single point of focus in AF mode or a point of focus in manual focus mode.

- ❖ From 117 focus points arranged in a 9 by 13 grid, select one. This option gives you greater control over how you frame your images and where you want to concentrate by distributing a ring-mode number of focus points around the screen.
- ❖ Choose from 425 focal points that are arranged in a grid of 17 by 25. This option gives you greater control over the composition and more accurate focus by scattering more focus points over the screen. It works especially well for photographing subjects in difficult or detailed environments.

Your shooting style, the subject matter you photograph, and the level of focus precision you need will all influence which of these alternatives you choose. The 425-point option can be your best choice if you often take pictures in challenging conditions or need to be very accurate with your focus. The 117-point option, however, can be enough if you're looking for a more straightforward and approachable focusing technique.

PRE-AF

When PRE-AF is activated, focusing is always successful. The camera will continue to change the focus even if you do not push the shutter button all the way. You could anticipate that this option would use a lot more battery power since the AF motor is always running. Theoretically, this mode could improve concentration. However, it doesn't seem to have any effect. Because it shortens battery life, this setting need to be disabled.

AF ILLUMINATOR

If you select this option, the camera will turn on the AF ILLUMINATOR anytime you need to focus in the dark. There will be increased contrast between the LED light and your subject, potentially allowing the camera to focus more successfully in low light. Remember that the light's range is restricted, thus it will not work for faraway subjects. Also, if you're filming in secret or someplace where the light will distract your subjects, you probably don't want it on. Trying to concentrate by hand is probably the best choice in this scenario. People routinely ask me why I keep my cameras switched on when they are not being utilized.

FACE/EYE DETECTION SETTING

The camera will position the face in front of the background and change the exposure and focus settings when it detects a face. You may also choose which eye the camera focuses on when face recognition is turned on.

❖ When FACE DETECTION is turned on, the camera can identify faces in photos thanks to Intelligent Face Detection. Additionally, you may adjust the eye recognition parameters.

➢ **Eye off:** Focus on identifying faces rather than specific eyes.

➢ **EYE AUTO:** When a face is identified, this feature will choose the eye to concentrate on automatically.

➢ PRIORITY FOCUS IS GIVEN TO THE RIGHT EYE OF FOCUS.

➢ **LEFT EYE PRIORITY:** When a person is gazing, their left eye is given precedence.

➢ **OFF:** The Intelligent Face Detection and Eye Priority settings are turned off.

Depending on your shooting technique and subject arrangement, you may adjust how the camera recognizes and focuses on faces with these unique settings. Using face and eye recognition might help you keep your subjects' features in great focus every time, especially if you shoot a lot of group or portrait photographs.

➢ The face may not show up in the green portion of the picture if the subject moves while the shutter is pressed.

➢ Some camera settings provide the ability to change the exposure of the whole frame, not just the subject.

➢ SUBJECT DETECTION SETTING will be instantly disabled when Intelligent Face Detection is enabled with FACE DETECTION ON.

Take note:

❖ In the focus zone, a white frame will appear around a face.

❖ From among many focus locations, the camera will automatically choose one face.

❖ Touch the screen and move the focus area to change the topic. You may also utilize the focus stick, often known as the focus handle, if WIDE is chosen as the AF MODE.

❖ When the camera is focused on one eye, press the RIGHT/LEFT EYE flip function button to flip between them.

❖ When the person returns to the frame, the camera will wait. When no face is visible, a white frame could show up instead.

❖ Following a burst shooting, face-picking may cease, depending on the firing circumstances.

❖ Faces in all orientations—up, down, and sideways—can be recognized by the camera.

❖ The camera will automatically focus on the subject's face when their eyes are obscured by hair, glasses, or other objects.

SETTING FOR SUBJECT DETECTION

You may choose whether the camera should give certain topic types—like automobiles or animals—more weight when altering the focus.

❖ **SUBJECT Spotting ON:** It is necessary to allow subject detection for certain topic kinds. One of the following choices is yours:

➢ **ANIMAL:** Helps cats and dogs concentrate better.

➢ **BIRD:** Concentrate on birds and insects.

➢ **AUTOMOBILE:** Identifies and monitors automobiles, particularly those engaged in racing.

➢ Makes it possible for cyclists and motorcyclists to concentrate and obey instructions.

➢ Identifies and tracks drones and airplanes by concentrating on their bodies, heads, and cockpits.

➢ **TRAIN:** Focused on identifying and tracking train front ends or driver cabins.

❖ **OFF:** Turns off topic identification. These options enhance your ability to produce crisp, well-focused images in a variety of shooting scenarios by letting you tailor subject tracking to specific shot types. Select the appropriate topic type for both the ring location and the subjects you are capturing to get the best possible results.

➢ FACE/EYE DETECTION is disabled while SUBJECT DETECTION ON is enabled.

➢ A white frame will be used to identify the topic in the focal area.

➢ Among the many subjects in the focus region, the camera will automatically choose one.

➢ Touch the screen and move the focus area to change the topic. You may also utilize the focus stick, often known as the focus handle, if WIDE is chosen as the AF MODE.

➢ When the person returns to the frame, the camera will wait. Consequently, there may be times when the white frame appears in areas where the intended subject type is obscured.

➢ Following a burst of shots, subject recognition may stall, depending on the shooting circumstances.

➢ Regardless of inclination (horizontal or vertical), the camera can detect objects.

AF+MF

AF+MF is a highly handy and powerful tool. If you keep your finger on the shutter halfway down after autofocusing, you may manually change the focus by twisting the focus ring. This setting offers a huge advantage when focused. Modern AF systems are highly effective, however they may be fooled. Suppose you wish to photograph a subject, like a flower or bird, that is obscured by a thick leaf canopy. The trees in front of your subject should not be picked up by the camera's autofocus system. With the AF+MF option, you may manually focus on the last 10% after utilizing AF to get 90% of the way there. The LCD will zoom in on the area you've selected to focus on when you do the aforementioned while using SINGLE AF and AF-S with the FOCUS CHECK feature enabled. This will make it even easier for you to concentrate. Just turning the command dial on the back of the camera will alter the zoom from 6x to 2.5x. The picture below shows how the autofocus system was fooled into focusing on the raging water just behind the duck's back. The ducks are slightly out of focus, which is obviously not what I want.

To get the highlights to land on the ducks, I could have used the focus ring to dial them back somewhat while AF+MF was on. Because it may be helpful in a number of circumstances, I advise you to always have AF+MF on.

Focus Zoom AF + MF

The focus ring may be rotated to zoom in on the current focus zone when SINGLE POINT is selected for AF MODE and ON under AF/MF SETTING > FOCUS CHECK. The zoom ratio may be adjusted via the rear command dial.

MF ASSIST

Choose the focus display method in fixed focus mode.
- ❖ **The DIGITAL SPLIT** picture option will show a split picture in the center of the frame, either black or white (MONOCHROME) or color (COLOR). When applying manual focus, the split-image area will be employed to frame the subject. After that, adjust the focus ring until the split image's four components are correctly aligned. This indicates that you are focused on your topic.
- ❖ **DIGITAL MICROPRISM:** This option shows a grid pattern to emphasize blur when your subject is out of focus. When you manually shift the focus, the blur pattern goes away. The pattern gives way to a distinct picture as your topic comes into focus. Your topic is in the proper focus position when you see this visual cue.
- ❖ **FOCUS PEAK HIGHLIGHT:** Makes manual focusing easier by enhancing black lines. By selecting a hue and adjusting the growing intensity to your preference,

you may personalize the display. This feature helps you assess if your topic is in focus by emphasizing regions with high contrast.

❖ Shows focus without a visual help and turns off manual focus assistance. It's important to realize that MF (Manual Focus) cannot be used in this mode.

INTERLOCK FOCUS RING & MF ASSIST

Only when the focus ring is in manual focus mode will the MF ASSIST-set display show up if ON is selected.

FOCUS CHECK

You may manually focus with the back command dial. When you press it, the camera will zoom in, improving your perspective and focusing on your topic. The LCD will automatically zoom in on the chosen focus zone when you choose manual focus mode. Additionally, the FOCUS CHECK menu feature may be activated. (FOCUS CHECK was located in the SCREEN SET-UP menu inside a BLUE MENUS on older Fuji cameras.) The FOCUS CHECK feature may also be utilized with AF+MF settings while shooting in AF-S focusing mode. Once again, I usually have FOCUS PEAK HIGHLIGHT (RED HIGH) selected in my MF ASSIST menu. For me, this is the simplest and most efficient way to gauge how focused I am. The AF+MF option is essential, in my opinion, even if FOCUS CHECK might be difficult at times. Sometimes it's exactly what you need to concentrate on and works very well. Sometimes it might be annoying since you can't see the whole frame at once. To rapidly toggle it on and off as needed, you may wish to attach FOCUS CHECK to an Fn button on your camera or add it to your MY MENU.

INTERLOCK SPOT AE AND FOCUS AREA

Select ON to measure the current focus frame if SPOT or MULTI metering is enabled. This is quite straightforward to grasp. When you activate this feature while in SINGLE AF mode, your exposure meter is connected to the focus zone you specify, and the Spot Meter is selected as your measurement choice. I know exactly what to do. The focal point you have chosen should typically serve as the basis for your reading when using the Spot Meter. I always have this option enabled for this reason.

INSTANT AF SETTING

You may choose whether the camera uses single AF (AF S) or continuous AF (AF C) when you press a button in manual focus mode that is set to focus lock or AF-ON.

❖ AF-S (Single-Servo Auto Focus): The camera will only focus once if the autofocus button is only partially depressed. Until you release or completely push the shutter button to snap the picture, it will stay in focus. For taking pictures of still objects or concentrating on a particular topic before shooting, this mode is perfect.

❖ The camera shifts focus when the autofocus button is partially depressed while in AF-C (Continuous-Servo Autofocus) mode. Because the focus stays on the topic as it travels across the screen, this mode makes it simple to track moving subjects or capture fast-moving action. You may shoot crisp, clear pictures of moving situations by holding down the focusing button while the subject is hit.

Choose the proper autofocus mode for your shooting scenario, such as AF-S for precise focus or AF-C for ongoing autofocus tracking of moving objects.

Scale of Depth-Of-Field

The front of the XF14mm f/2.8, 16mm f/1.4, and 23mm f/1.4 lenses displays the depth of field (DOF) values. You can use an Electronic Depth-of-Field Scale if you don't have one of these lenses. To choose the depth of focus for photos that will be seen as copies, the book suggests utilizing the FILM FORMAT BASIS option, which has two possibilities. Use PIXEL BASIS to see your images in high quality on a digital screen.

Seeing how the science works here is incredible. In contrast to pixels that are properly sized and spaced out on an electronic display, it is based on how humans perceive the sharpness of liquid ink droplets that spread when put on paper. This slightly softer appearance, however, causes us to perceive a print from a distance as sharper than it actually is, even though the ink on paper is technically "blurrier." ("This effect is a little stronger on a print made from an original film image.") Consequently, the depth of field of the FILM FORMAT BASIS DOF scale is significantly greater than that of the PIXEL BASIS scale. But I wouldn't be too concerned about this setting. Put it on a pixel basis and put it out of your mind. Pretend it doesn't exist. In actuality, even if we print just a handful of the images, we still view every picture onscreen. I'm not a really meticulous pixel peeper, but I don't believe it has a big impact.

RELEASE/FOCUS PRIORITY

This option influences how the camera works in both AF-S and AF-C modes. If you set the priority to RELEASE, the shutter will fire even if the picture is not in focus. If you set the priority to FOCUS, the shutter will not fire until the camera is focused. This menu item enables you to give each AF-S and AF-C a distinct setting, swap them, or set them to the same value. I've been using cameras for a long time, and AF-S has always been set to FOCUS PRIORITY, while AF-C has always been set to RELEASE PRIORITY. I don't see any reason to alter this; thus I advise that you maintain these settings as they are.

AF RANGE LIMITER

- ❖ **OFF:** This option allows the camera to focus anywhere in its field of view by turning off the focus cap.
- ❖ **CUSTOM:** You may limit the focus to a certain range of distances using this option. The camera will only focus within the range you set for its lowest and maximum distances.
  - ➢ OK: This option verifies the range while concentrating just on the chosen distances.
  - ➢ The camera will adjust the focus limiter to the distance between two objects in the scene when you press the SET button.
- ❖ You may utilize the preset focus range settings quickly without having to manually configure them thanks to the PRESET1 and PRESET2 options. A certain length range is represented by each option.

The actual focus distance may vary from the settings specified and shown for the focus limiter. The following additional tasks may be done while choosing CUSTOM:
- ❖ Tap the touch display screen to choose the focus range.
- ❖ Rotate the focus ring rather than choosing an item on the screen to set the maximum focus distance to infinity.

In movie mode, all modifications made to this object will be reflected.

TOUCH SCREEN MODE

❖ **TOUCH SHOOTING:** Tap an object on the screen to focus it, and then press the shutter to capture a picture. Continuous burst picture capturing will take place as you keep your finger on the screen.

❖ **AF:** Touching the subject initiates the focusing process when autofocus is being used (S for AF-S or C for AF-C). The focus will remain in place once AF-S mode is enabled until you press the AF OFF button. Until you hit the AF OFF button, the camera will keep adjusting the focus in AF-C mode based on the subject's distance.

❖ **AF OFF:** You may utilize autofocus to focus on the selected subject by touching the screen while in manual focus mode (MF).

❖ **AREA:** Tap to choose a display area or focus point. Perfect focusing is ensured by the focus ring's ability to adapt to the proper position.

❖ **OFF:** Pressing this button disables the touchscreen control mode. After then, focusing and shooting are done using the standard settings.

CHAPTER EIGHT

ADVANCED SHOOTING MODES

SHOOTING SETTING

For still photos, change the shooting parameters. Click the (SHOOTING SETTING) tab on the picture shooting display, and then choose MENU/OK to examine the shooting settings.

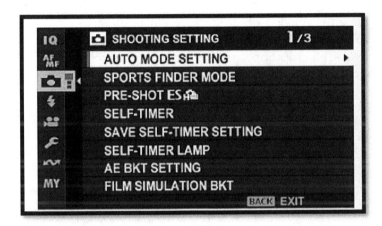

The Options Available

❖ AUTO MODE SETTING
❖ FILTER SETTING
❖ SPORTS FINDER MODE
❖ PRE-SHOT
❖ SELF-TIMER
❖ SAVE SELF-TIMER SETTING
❖ SELF-TIMER LAMP
❖ AE BKT SETTING
❖ FILM SIMULATION BKT
❖ FOCUS BKT SETTING
❖ PHOTOMETRY
❖ SHUTTER TYPE
❖ INTERVAL TIMER SHOOTING
❖ INTERVAL TIMER SHOOTING EXPOSURE SMOOTHING
❖ FLICKER REDUCTION
❖ FLICKERLESS S.S. SETTING
❖ IS MODE

- ❖ ISO
- ❖ DIGITAL TELE-CONV.
- ❖ WIRELESS COMMUNICATION

AUTOMODE SETTING

When the auto mode selection lever is in AUTO, choose a scene position.

SPORTS FINDER MODE

To capture pictures, use the crop in the center of the screen. If you want to take pictures of athletes, birds, or other moving objects, choose this option.
- ❖ **ON:** A 1.29× crop increases the lens's focal length by 1.29× while decreasing the picture angle. The crop appears as a frame on the screen.
- ❖ **OFF:** The crop of 1.29x is not in use.

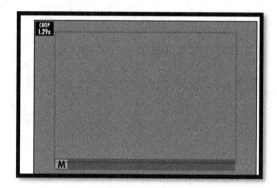

A setting known as IMAGE SIZE is available in the shooting menu. The sports finder does not have any settings that allow you to employ an electronic shutter.

PRE-SHOT

The camera uses the electronic shutter to begin shooting when the button is halfway pushed. This reduces the amount of time that passes between fully depressing the button and the picture being stored on the memory card. Shortly before the button is completely pushed, a series of pictures are stored.
- ❖ Flash photography is disabled while selecting ELECTRONIC SHUTTER in CH (high-speed burst) drive mode;
- ❖ Only pre-shot photography is enabled.

Self-timer

The self-timer is obvious. Off, two seconds, and ten seconds are its three settings. A little light on the front of the camera will flicker and count down as you push the shutter button. Additionally, all camera Q menus include this option. The self-timer shouldn't ever need to be configured via the settings menu. Never check your self-timer while browsing through alternatives, I'll repeat it again. The Q menu has it. Learn about the Q menu. Like the Fn buttons, the Q menu is a practical utility. Delay the shutter release.

- ❖ **2 SEC:** The shutter button is released after two seconds of pushing. to reduce the noise produced by the camera moving when the shutter is pushed. The self-timer light blinks when the timer goes off.
- ❖ **10 SEC:** The shutter is released after 10 seconds of pressing the button. Use it for photos when you want to seem authentic. The self-timer light blinks just before the picture is shot.
- ❖ **OFF:** Switch the self-timer off.

The timer will start when you completely press the shutter button if you choose anything other than OFF. The number of seconds till the shutter is released is shown on the display. Press DISP/BACK to stop the timer before you shoot the picture.

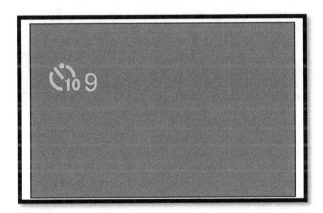

- ❖ Position yourself behind the camera to press the shutter button. Exposure and focus may be affected by standing in front of the lens.
- ❖ When the camera is switched off, the self-timer will instantly stop.

SAVE SELF-TIMER SETTING

The SELF-TIMER setting will remain active if you choose ON after turning off the camera.

Self-Timer Lamp

The self-timer bulb will illuminate during the self-timer shot if you choose ON. Use the OFF button to switch off the light while filming sequences at night or for other purposes.

INTERVAL TIMER SHOOTING

Select INTERVAL TIMER SHOOTING when using the X-M5 to take time-lapse pictures. You may adjust the start time, frame count, and shooting interval using this option. Choose

INFINITY for the frame count. The camera will be forced to continue shooting until the memory card is full as a result.

❖ Click MENU/OK after choosing INTERVAL TIMER SHOOTING from the SHOOTING SETTING menu.

❖ Click OK/MENU after selecting WITH IN-CAMERA TIMER. The settings for the interval timer will be shown.

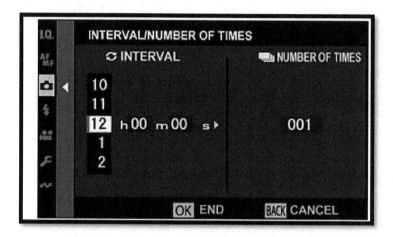

Select WITH EXTERNAL TIMER to operate a remote release with its own timer. After then, you'll be brought back to the picture screen, where you may begin interval-timer shooting by pressing the remote control.

❖ The focus stick, also known as the handle, regulates the quantity and duration of shots. To continue, press MENU/OK.

❖ Press MENU/OK after using the focus stick to specify a start time. It will start firing itself.

Naturally, you need to set your camera on a frame or track in order to record intervals. Regretfully, you are currently unable to simply transfer your interval from the camera to the video file. I've wanted Fuji to include this for a while; maybe a future firmware update will include it. Make sure the battery is completely charged and apply a strong battery hold before you start shooting. Use the CP-W126 DC coupler and the additional AC-9V AC power adapter for optimal performance during intervals. In between shots, the screen goes black and comes back up just before the next one. You may always hit the shutter button to restart it.

Interval Timer Shooting Exposure Smoothing

When using an interval timer, choose ON to ensure that the exposure changes quickly and doesn't significantly vary between images.

❖ If the subject's light fluctuates often, inconsistent exposure might happen. Use shorter INTERVAL TIMER SHOOTING > INTERVAL settings for subjects that shift significantly in brightness or darkness while being photographed.

❖ Select A (auto) sensitivity to use exposure smoothing in manual mode (mode M).

INTERVAL PRIORITY MODE

During interval-timer shooting, if ON is selected, the camera will adjust the shutter speed to avoid exposures lasting longer than the interval between frames. Only when the shutter speed is set to A (auto) does this option function.

AE BKT SETTING

Adjust the exposure bracketing parameters.

Frames/Step Settings

The number of photos you capture throughout the bracketing process is up to you. The exposure varies from photo to shot.
- ❖ FRAMES: Determine how many pictures are included in the bracketing arrangement.
- ❖ Step: For every photo, choose variable exposure.

1 Frame, Continuous

- ❖ 1 FRAME: Every bracketing picture is taken separately.
- ❖ CONTINUOUS: The bracketing sequence's shots are captured in a single explosion.

SEQUENCE SETTING: Decide which order to take the pictures.

FILM SIMULATION BKT

For bracketing, choose one of the three forms of film simulation that are offered.

FOCUS BKT SETTING

There are two focus bracketing options: AUTO and MANUAL.

PHOTOMETRY

Decide how exposure should be measured by the camera.

Shutter Type

The usual focal plane of the X-M5 All DSLRs and the great majority of other cameras ever made use the same kind of shutter, known as a MECHANICAL SHUTTER (MS). The sensor is then turned on and off by an ELECTRONIC SHUTTER (ES). In reality, the drapes don't open or shut. (First-generation cellphones do not have the electronic shutter capability.) This allows for quiet operation and shutter speeds of up to 1/32,000 seconds. When filming in a theater, on a set, or during a secret picture session when secrecy is necessary, this technique should be used. Additionally, the ES allows you to take pictures with wide apertures, something that mechanical shutters can't always do. In high light, this allows you to capture minuscule depths of field. Using my 56mm lens at f/1.2 over snowy fields in direct sunshine produced some interesting images. I will also use the ES when shooting straight into the sun. Be careful not to damage the camera's sensor or burn your eyes. (Avoid shooting in the middle of the day; instead, aim for the sun when it is quite low in the sky.)

You should be aware that artificial hair is not flawless and has limitations. The ES is incompatible with Flash. The ES is prone to distortion and banding issues while filming in very rapid speed.

You may choose MS+ES, ES+ES, or MS just. The mechanical shutter of your camera will be activated by pressing MS+ES until it reaches its maximum speed. It will then migrate to the ES without any problems. Make sure that at least one of the selections in your MY MENU is SHUTTER TYPE. For the most choices, leave your camera settings at MS+ES if you don't want to utilize Flash. The hot shoe won't work if the camera is set to ES.

FLICKER REDUCTION

FLICKER REDUCTION minimizes flicker in images and on the screen while using fluorescent lights or other comparable light sources.

- ❖ **ALL FRAMES:** Because flicker reduction applies to every frame, shooting continually lowers frame rate.
- ❖ **FIRST FRAME:** Flicker is only measured in the first frame, and all subsequent flashing frames have the same drop.
- ❖ **OFF:** Flicker mitigation is turned off.

It takes longer to shoot pictures when flicker reduction is turned on. Select FLICKER REDUCTION OFF while using the automatic shutter. Flicker reduction is impossible while filming a movie.

FLICKERLESS S.S. SETTING

Toggle ON and change the shutter speed to lessen flickering from LED lights and other sources. This feature is only available in modes S and M.

IS MODE

When shooting handheld at slower shutter rates, IS MODE reduces blur from camera shaking. Only lenses with optical image stabilization (OIS) can perform this function. When an OIS-compatible lens is attached, this menu choice will become green. What incredible OIS are offered by Fuji lenses? Even with long lenses, you'll be shocked at how low you can hold your camera and still get good pictures. **Look at these possibilities for IS Mode:**

- ❖ It is possible to modify the picture continuously. In this case, more electricity will be consumed.
- ❖ **SHOOTING ONLY:** Stabilization of images is only applicable while the shutter button is partially depressed or engaged.
- ❖ **(OFF):** The image correcting feature is not enabled. There is a little "shaking hand with a line through it" indication on the screen. This is the mode to utilize while using a tripod.

The +MOTION option has no effect when the sensitivity is fixed. Additionally, it may not be available in certain environments. Depending on the lighting and the object's speed, the effect might change. The value provided via IS MODE is superseded by the option chosen via the lens image stabilization switch, if any. You can hear camera noises or vibrations when image stabilization is in action.

Wireless Communication

Using this option, your camera may be connected to computers and phones running the FUJIFILM Camera Remote app. After connecting, you may use your phone to see and download the camera's pictures, remotely operate it, and provide the position of the camera so that your images can be geotagged. Although it is linked to a specific Wi-Fi or Fn button on all X Series cameras, this function may also be used via the PLAYBACK MENU when playing back photographs. You should either add Wireless Communication to your MY MENU for easy access or assign it to one of your Fn buttons if you utilize the Camera Remote app. Therefore, when you've taken a great picture and are eager to share it, you don't need to search for this thing in the alternatives. Another option is to just hit the Fn key.

CHAPTER NINE
STARTING OUT WITH VIDEO

About Video Recording and Playback

The Movie Recording

Make a sound recording of movies. You may record movies by turning the mode dial to [Vlog] or ![movie icon] (movie) or by clicking the ⊙ (movie recording) button.

❖ The ⊙ (Movie Recording) Button

❖ ![movie icon] (Movie) Mode

❖ [Vlog]

❖ Adjusting Movie Settings

The " ⊙ " button (Movie Recording)

When in still photography mode, you may quickly and conveniently record movies by pressing the ⊙ (movie recording) button.

Note: For focus mode, the camera automatically chooses [CONTINUOUS AF].

   A. To begin recording, press ⊙ .

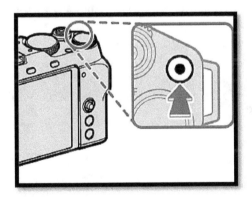

The recording will begin.
> ➤ When the recording begins, a sign is shown by the recording indicator symbol.
> ➤ The display borders become green for high-speed displays and red for movie recording.
> ➤ A count-up display shows how long the recording will last, and a count-down display shows how much time is left.

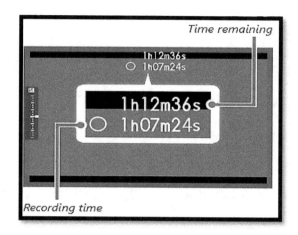

Press the button once more to stop the recording. When the memory card is full or the recording reaches its maximum duration, it pauses. Either an external microphone or the built-in microphone may be used to record sound. When recording, don't cover the microphone. Note that lens noise and other camera noises may be picked up by the microphone while recording. When photographing very bright scenes, streaks may be either vertical or horizontal. This is typical and does not indicate a problem. Turn the camera off when not in use and keep it out of direct sunlight to maximize recording duration. During recording, the indicator light illuminates the movie ring. You may choose whether the lamp blinks or remains steady, and whether it is an indication or AF-assist, by using the MOVIE SETTING > TALLY LIGHT option. During recording, adjust exposure by up to ±2 EV. Select OFF under MOVIE SETTING > REC FRAME INDICATOR to stop the borders of the movie display from changing color during recording. **Any of the following techniques may be used to adjust the recording's intensity and refocus:**

❖ Press the shutter button half-way.
❖ Press an "AF-ON" function button or
❖ Make use of the touch-sensitive keyboard.

A simulated horizon or histogram will show up if you hit the HISTOGRAM or ELECTRONIC LEVEL SWITCH buttons. While certain settings may not work while recording, others would not permit recording at all.

B. **To stop recording, press** ⊙ **once more:** When the memory card is full or the maximum duration is reached, recording automatically stops.

📹 (Movie) Mode

Rotate the mode dial to 📹 (movie) and use the shutter button to record movies for more control over camera settings.

❖ Select 📹 (movie) by using the mode dial.

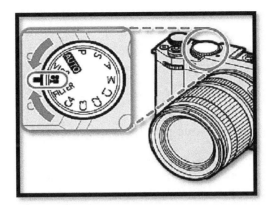

❖ **Start recording by pressing the shutter button.**

    ➢ While recording is underway, a recording indicator (⊙) is shown.

    ➢ When filming a movie, the display's borders glow red; when recording at high speed, they turn green.

    ➢ A countdown display indicates how much time is left, while a countup display indicates how long the recording is.

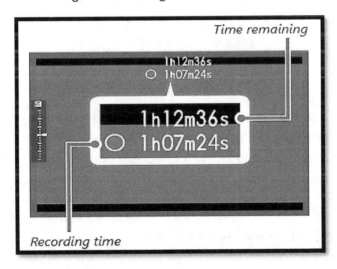

❖ **To stop recording, press the shutter button one more:** When the memory card is full or the maximum length is reached, recording automatically stops.

[Vlog]

The shutter button can be used to record movies at settings suitable for vlogs (video blogs) when the mode dial is turned to [Vlog]. Touch controls can be used to change settings.

❖ The settings used for recording movies in 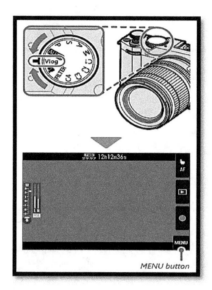 mode or with the ⊙ (movie recording) button are saved separately from those used in [Vlog] mode.

❖ Gestures using the touch function are not enabled.

Recording Vlogs

❖ To access [Vlog], turn the mode dial.

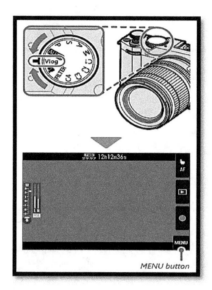

MENU button

➢ The shooting display for the vlog mode emerges.
➢ **Click the MENU button to see the shooting settings.**

   ▪ To go back to the shooting display, tap ⊠.
   ▪ Holding down the Play back button will bring up full-frame playback.

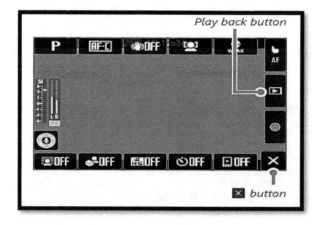

Play back button

⊠ button

130

❖ **Press the REC button or shutter to begin recording.**

- While recording is underway, a recording indicator (⊙) is shown.
- When filming a movie, the display's borders glow red; when recording at high speed, they turn green.
- A countdown display indicates how much time is left, while a countup display indicates how long the recording is.

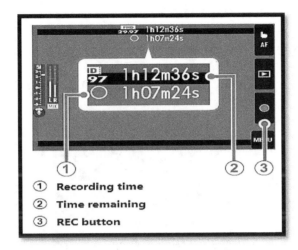

① **Recording time**
② **Time remaining**
③ **REC button**

❖ **Press the button once more to stop the recording:** When the memory card is full or the maximum length is reached, recording automatically stops.

The Shooting Display in Vlog Mode

When the LCD monitor is in vlog mode, vlog recording indicators show up.

❖ Touch zoom[1]
❖ MENU button[2]
❖ Touch screen mode[2]

131

❖ Vlog shooting mode
❖ Play back button[2]
❖ Mic level

Notes:
❖ Only appears when a touch zoom lens is attached.
❖ Whenever touch zoom is enabled, it is not seen.

Modifying the Configuration

Tap the MENU button to see the shooting settings. To see the configuration options, tap

each item. Touch the shooting display, push the ▣ button, or tap a selected item to hide the configuration options.

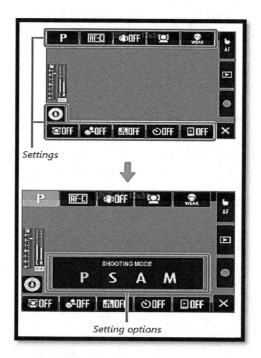

The settings listed below are modifiable.
❖ [SHOOTING MODE]

❖ 🎥 [FOCUS MODE]

❖ 🎥 [IS MODE]

❖ 🎥 [FACE/EYE DETECTION SETTING]

❖ 🎥 [PORTRAIT ENHANCER LV]

132

❖ [BACKGROUND DEFOCUS MODE]
❖ [PRODUCT PRIORITY MODE]
❖ [HIGH SPEED REC]
❖ 📹 [SELF-TIMER]
❖ [9:16 SHORT MOVIE MODE]
❖ [MICROPHONE DIRECTION SETTING]

Design notes

❖ By choosing [ON] for [BACKGROUND DEFOCUS MODE], the aperture is fixed at the lens's widest setting.
❖ When filming a product review, for instance, choose [ON] for [PRODUCT PRIORITY MODE] to keep the camera focused on an object in the foreground.
❖ The built-in microphone or an optional external microphone is used to record sound. When recording, avoid covering the microphone.
❖ Be aware that during recording, the microphone may pick up sounds produced by the camera, including lens noise.
❖ Movies with extremely light topics may show vertical or horizontal streaks. This is not a sign of a fault; it is normal.
❖ **To get the most out of the recording time:**
   ▪ As much as possible, keep the camera out of direct sunlight, and whenever it is not in use, switch it off.
❖ During movie recording, the indicator lamp illuminates. You can select whether the lamp is an indicator or AF-assist and whether it blinks or stays constant by using the 📷 [MOVIE SETTING] > [TALLY LIGHT] option. If the lens has a zoom ring, you can use it to modify the zoom and change exposure compensation by up to ±2 EV while recording.
❖ To stop the display's borders from changing color while a video is being recorded, choose [OFF] for 📷 [video SETTING] > 📹 [REC FRAME INDICATOR].
❖ **As the recording is going on, you can:**
   ▪ Modify the sensitivity
   ▪ Exposure Compensation
   ▪ **Use any of the following techniques to refocus:**
      ➤ Halfway press the shutter button.
      ➤ Press a function button that has the designation [AF-ON] attached to it.
      ➤ Make use of touch screen controllers.
   ▪ Press the button that has been assigned to [HISTOGRAM] or [ELECTRONIC LEVEL SWITCH] to display a histogram or artificial horizon.
❖ In certain situations, settings might not apply when recording, while in others, recording might not be possible.

❖ Using the focus stick (focus lever) and rear command dial pick ⬛ [AF/MF SETTING] > [FOCUS AREA] to select the focus area for filming.

About Temperature Warnings

When the camera's or the battery's temperature increases, it immediately shuts off to protect itself. Image noise may increase if a temperature warning is shown. Before turning the camera on again, turn it off and let it cool.

Making Use of an External Microphone

Sound recording is possible with external microphones that attach to 3.5 mm diameter jacks; plug-in mics are not compatible. For more information, consult the microphone manual.

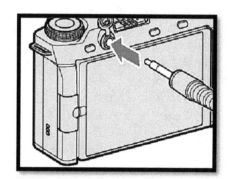

Adapters for the XLR microphone

TEAC TASCAM CA-XLR2d-F XLR microphone adapters are compatible with the camera. Go to the TASCAM website to learn more.

Changing the Movie's Settings

Movie settings can be changed using the MOVIE SETTING item in the picture or movie menus.
❖ Select the MOVIE SETTING item from the photo menu and press the MOVIE RECORDING RELEASE button to quickly adjust the movie recording parameters.
❖ Press the shutter button and select "MOVIE" from the drive-mode menu to begin filming.
❖ In MOVIE MODE, you can change parameters like frame rate and size.
❖ Among other things, you can alter the file type, bit rate, and location by using MEDIA REC SETTING.
❖ The focus mode is selected by the focus mode switch.   The camera will automatically switch to C if either FACE DETECTION ON or SUBJECT DETECTION

ON is set under AF/MF SETTING > FACE/EYE DETECTION SETTING or SUBJECT DETECTION SETTING. However, note that pressing M when FACE DETECTION ON or SUBJECT DETECTION ON is selected turns off the ability to recognize faces and subjects.

The movie options will change if you make any changes to the photo menus using the MOVIE SETTING item. The other set of choices is immediately updated as you make changes to one. The option chosen under BMOVIE SETTING > MEDIA REC SETTING determines the kind of memory card that is supported.

❖ 360 Mbps bit-rate movies can be recorded by video cards with a Video Speed Class of V60 or above.

❖ Movies with bit rates of 100 or 200 Mbps can be recorded on UHS Speed Class 3 or higher cards.

The depth of field

To soften the background, open the aperture as much as you can. Aperture can be manually changed at values other than A. To make background details softer, use low f-numbers. When [APERTURE PRIORITY AE] or [MANUAL] is chosen for [MOVIE SETTING] > [SHOOTING MODE], aperture can be changed.

About Viewing Movies

You may watch movies with the camera. You'll see a sign next to the movie once you've chosen it and pressed the PLAY button to start playing it. To start the movie, press the focus stick, also known as the focus lever.

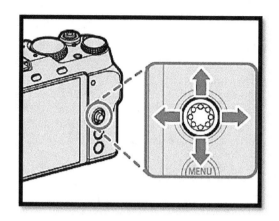

Focus stick (focus lever)	Full-frame playback	Playback in progress (▶)	Playback paused (⏸)
Up	View photo information	End playback	
Down	Start playback	Pause playback	Start/resume playback
Left/right	View other pictures	Adjust speed	Single frame rewind/advance

During playback, progress is displayed on the screen.

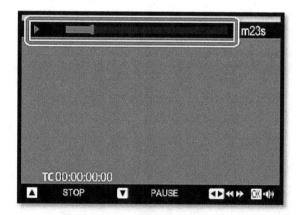

❖ Avoid covering the speaker while it is playing.
❖ To pause playback and show the volume controls, press [MENU/OK]. To change the volume, move the focus stick, also known as the focus lever, up or down. To start playing again, press [MENU/OK]. 🄵 [SOUND SET-UP] > [PLAYBACK VOLUME] is another way to change the volume.

❖ Press ▶️ button to watch movies on a TV that is linked via HDMI rather than the camera monitor.

About Playback Speed

To change the playback speed while it is playing, press the focus stick (also known as the focus lever) to the left or right. The number of arrows (▶ or ◀) indicates speed.

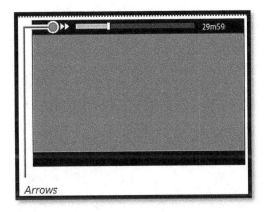

Arrows

Viewing Movies While Vlog Recording

By rotating the mode dial to [Vlog], you can hit ▶️ on the screen to see your most recent shot.

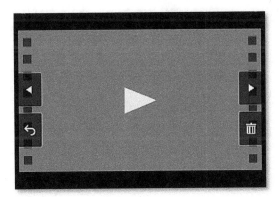

❖ To start playing, tap the screen.
❖ To choose different shots, tap ◀ or ▶ .
❖ Tap 🗑 to remove the current shot.

❖ The most recently viewed item will be shown if you have viewed any other items since your last shoot.

During playback, tapping ▤ will display the playback controls.

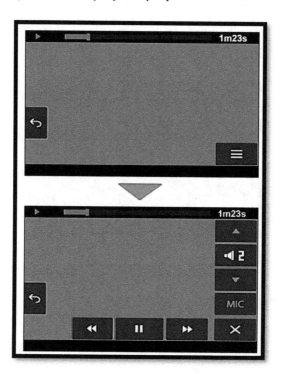

Control		Function
⏸	**Pause**	Pause playback. Tap again to resume.
⏩ **⏪**	**Advance/ rewind**	Rewind or advance the movie. When playback paused, you can tap these buttons to rewind or advance a frame at a time.
▲ **▼**	**Volume**	Adjust playback volume.
MIC	**Channel selection**	Adjust audio settings for use when viewing 4ch movies.
✕	**Close**	Hide movie playback controls.
↺	**Back**	End playback and return to the shooting display.

During playback, there is no way to change the volume or choose the channel. To utilize these controls, pause the playback.

THE MOVIE SETTING

Modify the movie recording settings. To view recording choices, choose the (MOVIE SETTING) tab under the movie shooting option. All you have to do is hit MENU/OK.

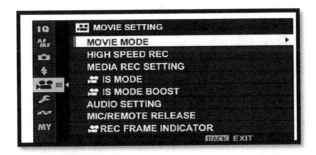

The Options Available

❖ MOVIE MODE
❖ HIGH SPEED REC
❖ MEDIA REC SETTING
❖ IS MODE
❖ IS MODE BOOST
❖ AUDIO SETTING
❖ MIC/REMOTE RELEASE
❖ FREC FRAME INDICATOR

THE MOVIE MODE

Establish the aspect ratio, frame rate, and frame size prior to filming.
    ❖ Select MOVIE SETTINGS from the shooting menu. Next, select MOVIE MODE and press MENU/OK.
    ❖ Set the required frame size and aspect ratio (A) by moving the focus stick (focus handle) up or down, and then move it to the right.

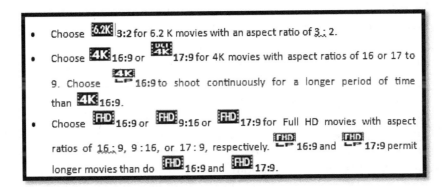

❖ Select a frame rate (B) by dragging the focus stick (focus handle) up or down, and then press MENU/OK.

BACKGROUND DEFOCUS MODE

Regardless of the user's choices, if ON is selected, the camera will automatically set the aperture to the lowest f-stop (maximum aperture). Only when the mode dial is in the Vlog position does this option become active.

HIGH SPEED REC

Make high-framerate videos. You might observe details or fast-moving objects that are impossible to see with the human eye when watching high-frame-rate footage in slow motion. You can customize the recording and playback rates if you select ON. To capture just external recordings connected via HDMI, select ON HDMI just. You are unable to select a 200P or 240P recording frame rate in this situation. Additionally, remember that the playback frame rate cannot be altered.

MEDIA REC SETTING

Select the location, file format, and compression for the movie file.

The destination

Choose between the options for saving movies and where you wish to play and save them.

File Format and Compression

Choose the kind of movie file and the compression method.
❖ A portable compressed file format is H.264 420 MOV. 8-bit depth video is recorded using 4:2:0 chroma sub-sampling and long GOP interframe compression.
❖ H.264 420 MP4: A suitable file format for online movie streaming.
❖ Compared to H.264, the H.265 420 MOV format compresses files more effectively. Video with a 10-bit depth is recorded using 4:2:0 chroma subsampling and long GOP interframe compression.
❖ Compared to H.264, the H.265 422 MOV format compresses data more efficiently. Video with a 10-bit depth is recorded using 4:2:2 chroma subsampling and long GOP interframe compression.

NOTE:
❖ 4:2:2 chroma subsampling is utilized when sending video over HDMI to an external device. While other video formats are supplied at a 10-bit depth, H.264 video is transmitted at an 8-bit depth.

- ❖ Long GOP achieves the ideal ratio of image quality to high compression. It's an excellent option for longer photos because of its adorable files.
- ❖ Choose F-Log/HLG RECORDING, HIGH SPEED REC, or MOVIE MODE to change the file format and compression.

IS MODE

Choose the image stabilization mode.
- ❖ In-Body Image Stabilization (IB IS) should be enabled.
- ❖ Make sure your camera has both DIS and IBIS image stabilization enabled. Depending on the MOVIE MODE choice used, the crop changes. To lessen excessive camera shake, use this option.
- ❖ **OFF:** Turns image stabilization on and off.

IS MODE BOOSTING?

Choose the picture stabilization level.

TIME CODE SETTING (Recording Movies)

When recording movies, adjust the time code display options (hour, minute, second, and frame number). Press MENU/OK on the movie shooting screen, and then choose the (TIME CODE SETTING) option to view the time code settings.

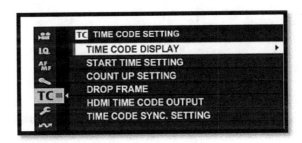

- ❖ TIME CODE DISPLAY
- ❖ START TIME SETTING
- ❖ COUNT UP SETTING
- ❖ DROP FRAME
- ❖ HDMI TIME CODE OUTPUT
- ❖ TIME CODE SYNC. SETTING

Time code display

Turn ON to show time figures when a movie is being recorded, played back, and dubbed.

START TIME SETTING

Select the time number that determines the current time.
- ❖ MANUAL INPUT: Select the start time by hand.
- ❖ Present TIME: Assign the present instant as the start time.
- ❖ Set the time back to 0:00.

COUNT UP SETTING

You can choose if the time is recorded continuously or just while the video is being recorded.
- ❖ REC RUN: Timed when the film was being recorded.
- ❖ Free Run: Time is continuously tracked.

DROP FRAME

The time code (in seconds) and recording time (in fractions of a second) will quickly diverge at frame rates of 59.94P and 29.97P. In order to synchronize the recording time with the time code, you can indicate whether the camera will lose frames as necessary.
- ❖ **ON:** To ensure accurate time coding and recording, enable frame-dropping.
- ❖ **OFF:** There are no dropped frames.

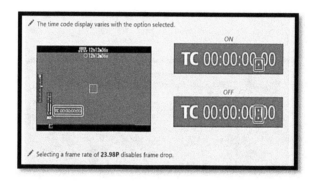

HDMI TIMECODE OUTPUT

Select if you want time codes to be sent to HDMI devices.

TIME CODE SYNC SETTING

Select whether to use an external device to synchronize time codes.

Connect to the ATOMOS AirGlu BT

The camera syncs time codes and connects to related external devices if you select ON. The smartphone icon appears on the screen in yellow since it is not possible to connect to a smartphone at the same time.

CHAPTER TEN

UNDERSTANDING PLAYBACK AND PLAYBACK MENU

You can see and edit a photo in the replay menu after capturing it. This menu allows you to explore images by zooming in to verify focus, searching through your photos, and removing undesired images, among other things. You can also manage and edit your photos directly on the camera with features like image rating, slideshow playback, and RAW conversion.

Playback Display

The indicators that could appear during playback are listed in this section. Displays are presented with all indicators lit for illustrative purposes.

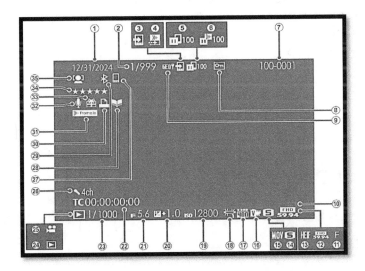

1. Date and time
2. Frame number display
3. Image transfer order
4. Frame.io image transfer order
5. Image transfer status
6. Frame.io upload progress
7. Frame number
8. Protected image
9. Location data
10. Low battery

11. Image quality
12. Movie mode
13. HEIF
14. Image size
15. Film format
16. Film simulation
17. Dynamic range
18. White balance
19. Sensitivity
20. Exposure compensation
21. Aperture
22. Time code
23. Shutter speed
24. Playback mode indicator
25. Movie icon
26. Four-channel (quadrophonic) audio
27. Bluetooth host
28. Photobook assist indicator
29. Bluetooth ON/OFF
30. DPOF print indicator
31. Frame.io connection status
32. Voice memo
33. Gift image
34. Rating
35. Face detection indicator

Fundamental Operation

First and foremost: click the PLAYBACK button!

The Playback Button

You can touch your photos to view them. It sounds like a great time. You can set up multiple playback buttons on your camera. I now use my AF-L ring as a second playback button to make it easier for me to see photographs when I'm shooting with one hand, as when I'm on a bike, driving, or flying. I no longer need to push the PLAYBACK button with my left hand. I can press the second button with my thumb instead. Playback can be controlled by each button. If you desired, you may have three playback buttons. or four. maybe seven. Well, perhaps not seven.

Scrolling

There are several ways you can see your photos. The easiest way to scroll is via the front command dial. You can also use the AF joystick and the buttons on the left and right thumb pads. Turn the back command dial to the left to view more than one picture at once. Nine images are displayed in a grid when the ring is clicked once. The process of creating a 100-frame grid only requires two clicks. You can use any of the aforementioned methods to navigate your thumbnails while viewing them in any grid layout. Pressing the OK button or key will cause the image to appear in full-size view. You can then spin the rear command dial to return to the grid or scroll indefinitely. Use the back command dial to zoom in and examine the sharpness of your photos. The image will zoom to the location of the focus zone you have chosen when you capture the picture when you tap. It will zoom back to the full screen if you press it again. The back command dial allows you to zoom in and out. I advise using the "press or double-tap" options instead, though, as they are far quicker.

RAW Image Zooming

If you are only shooting RAW, you should be aware that zooming closer won't give you a realistic picture of how crisp your images are. The reason behind this is that the JPEG pictures that come with RAW files are only medium in size. They are insufficiently large. (This applies to every camera.) Because of this, your photos might not be as clear when downloaded and viewed on a large screen, even if they are sharp when zoomed in. Use RAW+JPEG with IMAGE SIZE set to L3:2 and IMAGE QUALITY set to RAW if you want to shoot in RAW. In addition to a JPEG of the original image, you can zoom in to see sharpness better when you attach a full-size JPEG to your RAW file.

Because your photos are smaller and have already been processed to achieve the desired look—at least partially because of the FILM SIMULATION you chose and any additional camera settings you may have used—sharing them is also made easier. The FUJIFILM Camera Remote software allows you to share JPEGs quickly and conveniently, but it does not allow you to download RAW data. Your JPEGs may look fantastic most of the time, but you will still have RAW files, which offer more editing possibilities and a larger dynamic range. It's so good that you might determine that working with your RAW data on your computer is not as good as getting the JPEG straight from the camera.

The button for DISP/BACK

During playback, the indicator display is controlled by the DISP/BACK button.

This button provides four view options when in playback mode:
- ❖ Full-size images with shooting information are the standard; full-sized images without shooting information are the exception. **Clean and tidy!**
- ❖ INFO: All shooting details are included in the snapshot image.
- ❖ Favorites: A full-size photo with the time, date, image number, and "Favorites" or star rating should be included. The current image can be rated from 0 to 5 stars using the up and down arrow buttons.
- ❖ Little star icons in the upper left corner will show pictures with star ratings while the video is playing in both the STANDARD and FAVORITES views. The format in which these star ratings are stored is exclusive to Fuji. They are not the same as the conventional star rating information used by the great majority of photo processing software. At the moment, they are limited to the camera and cannot be moved to other shooting applications. That's right; there is cause for alarm. If you could email them to Lightroom, it would be fantastic. The procedure would be streamlined and expedited as a result. There is an alternative, though.

Viewing Photographic Information

The photo information is shown differently as you push the focus stick, also known as the focus handle, upward.

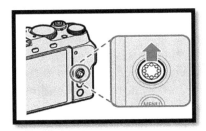

Focus Point Zooming in

Press the focus stick (or handle) in the center to approach the focus spot. Simply press the button once more to return to full-frame playback.

Viewing the Picture

You may select between full-frame, playback zoom, and multi-frame playback modes using the command dial on the back of the camera. Rotating the rear command dial to the left or right causes the display to change. The display shifts backward when you turn the dial in the opposite direction.

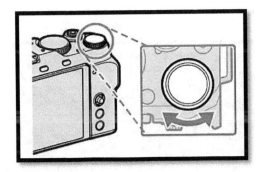

- Playback Zoom
- Multi-Frame Playback

Playback Zoom

Turn the back command dial to the left to view a larger image, and to the right to view a smaller image. Press the middle of the back command dial, MENU/OK, or DISP/BACK to exit Zoom. The maximum zoom ratio changes depending on the IMAGE SIZE > IMAGE QUALITY SETTING option selected.

Multi-frame playback

To adjust how many photos are shown, turn the back command dial to the left when a picture is in full frame.
- Use the focus stick to select the desired image, and then click MENU/OK to view it in full-frame.
- You can move the focus stick up or down to see more images on the screens with nine and one hundred frames.

A shortcut

If you haven't chosen a card yet, double-click the key to fast switch to the other card. Pressing the button on any of these cameras will take you straight to the PLAYBACK MENU. Holding down the PLAY button will play it again.

Very Important Caution!

Pressing the key after choosing an item from the PLAYBACK MENU will return you to that menu item. If you double-click the joystick, it will immediately try to connect to your INSTAX printer, assuming you made an INSTAX print the last time you were in the PLAYBACK MENU.

About Playback Menu

Adjust the playback parameters. The playback menu display will appear when you press MENU/OK while in playback mode.

- RAW CONVERSION
- HEIF TO JPEG/TIFF CONVERSION
- ERASE
- CROP
- RESIZE
- PROTECT
- IMAGE ROTATE
- VOICE MEMO SETTING
- RATING
- TRANSFER IMAGE TO SMARTPHONE
- WIRELESS COMMUNICATION
- SLIDE SHOW
- PHOTOBOOK ASSIST
- PRINT ORDER (DPOF)
- instax PRINTER PRINT
- DISP ASPECT

The Raw Conversion

You can use this application to instantly save RAW photos from your camera as JPEGs. What distinguishes this from simply taking RAW+JPEG photos? This program is quite helpful because it allows you to use a variety of shooting choices on the new file. You can alter the exposure, white balance, highlight and shadow tones, and even the color scheme when converting. Additionally, you receive a Fuji FILM SIMULATION color that corresponds to the RAW transfers and your camera. Although they don't always work, the majority of RAW conversion software can approximate Fuji's color reproduction. What if you took a stunning RAW (or RAW+JPEG) picture with the VELVIA film sim? Even though you might like the picture, you could also prefer to see it in black and white or with a shade of white instead of daylight. You could want to add extra gloss or intensify the shadows. There are several options available to you. or every one of them. What if you want one with grain, one with deeper shadows, and one in black and white? Any RAW image can be converted into any JPEG image you like, and each is stored on your memory card as a distinct file. For photographers who exclusively shoot in RAW but still wish to share their work via the FUJIFILM app on their phones, this is really helpful. You only get a JPEG copy of every picture when you shoot RAW+JPEG, but you can only select and modify the RAW files you wish. After selecting an image and playing it back, click OK to open the PLAYBACK MENU and make your changes. The second choice from the bottom is this one. It's considerably quicker: simply press the Q button to display the panel while an image is being played back. After making the desired adjustments, click the Q button to see a preview of the updated image. You may either hit Q again to save the image or use the BACK button to undo the change. It's as easy as adding ice cream to a plate. Note: You can reload the RAW file onto a memory card and then into the camera as long as you have the original. To process the file once more, bring it back into the

RAW CONVERSION menu. The file will be recognized by your Fuji as a valid kind. **The following options are available for use:**

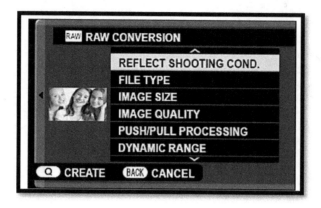

- GRAIN EFFECT
- WHITE BALANCE
- WB SHIFT
- HIGHLIGHT TONE
- SHADOW TONE
- COLOR
- SHARPNESS
- NOISE REDUCTION
- LENS MODULATION OPTIMIZER
- COLOR SPACE

Converting HEIF to JPEG/TIFF

Convert HEIF photos to TIFF or JPEG.

SELECT IMAGES

Select HEIF images to convert.

FILE FORMATS

Choose a format for the photos that have been converted.

THE ERASE

Using the TRASH button on the back of your camera, you can remove pictures. To remove one or more photos, you can alternatively select the PLAYBACK MENU and utilize the ERASE command. After selecting ERASE, you can either remove the current picture

(FRAME), remove a selection of photographs (SELECTED FRAMES), or remove all unprotected frames. On camera, deleted photos cannot be recovered. Don't worry, though. You'll get one last "OK?" alert before any pictures are deleted. Keep take mind that you can always use the shutter or DISP/BACK buttons to back out.

CROP

Any image can be cropped and stored on the memory card using this option. To display the PLAYBACK MENU, select the picture you wish to crop and click OK. To locate the exact area you wish to preserve, you can zoom in and out of the picture using the motion buttons and command dial on the rear of the camera. Click OK to bring up the confirmation option. Click OK once more to save the cropped image as a separate file. Keep in mind that your altered photo will always have a 3:2 aspect ratio, regardless of how much you zoom in. Additionally, the size will be shown as M or S. The cropped image will be "640," suitable for a 4x6 print, if you zoom in and the selections in the dialog box turn yellow.

RESIZE

Selecting this option allows you to save a reduced size of the selected image. There are three RESIZE options available in the PLAYBACK MENU: M, S, and 640. This suggests that you are using L image size. If you're shooting M or S, you might see other selections.) To save the image as a separate file, adjust its size and click OK.

PROTECT

You can guard against accidentally erasing picture files from your memory card. Choose from the options below.
   ❖ **FRAME:** Protect specific images. Select left or right to view your photos, and then MENU/OK to lock and unlock individual photos one at a time. Press the shutter button or DISP/BACK to end the procedure.
   ❖ **SET ALL:** will lock down each picture on the card.
   ❖ **RESET ALL:** This takes security off of every picture on the card.
Protected images are identified by a small "key" icon at the top of the frame while viewing them in STANDARD mode. Owners of protected photos are unable to remove, transfer, or assign star ratings to them. Please be aware that all of the photographs on your memory card, even those that are marked as private, will be erased when you format it.

IMAGE ROTATE

To rotate your photographs, select this menu item from the PLAYBACK MENU. Select an image, click ROTATE, and then follow the instructions to rotate it. Protected photographs cannot be moved.

VOICE MEMO SETTING

You may use this feature to turn any photograph into a 30-second audio memo. Click OK once you've chosen Voice Memo Recording from the Playback Menu. Then go back to your pictures. Press and hold the front command dial until the small "red dot" image light illuminates while you are looking at the image you want. It only takes a second, so have patience. Holding down the button will allow you to speak. Create any kind of noise you like, including sound effects and music. Release turns off the front command dial after you're finished. The voice memo can now be played again. A small "voice memo" icon will appear above the image when it is played again. To listen to your voice note, just turn the front command dial. Holding it down is not required for playback. To delete the previous message, just press and hold the command dial once more before recording a new one.

Playing Voice Memos

During playback, voice memo graphics are displayed using 🎤 **icons.**
  ❖ To play a note, select the photo by pressing the center of the front command dial.
  ❖ A progress meter will appear while the message plays again.
Use MENU/OK to pause playback, and then slide the focus stick (focus lever) up and down to change the volume. Press MENU/OK to start playback again. By selecting DSOUND SETUP > PLAYBACK VOLUME, you may also adjust the volume.

RATING

To rank photos, use stars.
  ❖ Select RATING from the playback menu.
  ❖ Twist the front command dial to choose a picture. To select a rating between 0 and 5 stars, use the command dial on the back. To select an image, you are not required to use the front command dial. Use a focus stick (or lever) instead. Additionally, you can press the AEL/AFL button to view the scoring display while single-frame, nine-frame, or hundred-frame playback is underway. Use the touch tools to zoom in or out. Ratings are not applicable to:
  ❖ Secured images
  ❖ Movies
  ❖ "Gift" photos, or images captured with other cameras

IMAGE TRANSFER TO SMARTPHONE

  ❖ **Select images to send via Bluetooth to a tablet or smartphone that is linked.**
    ▪ Select IMAGE & TRANSFER under TRANSFER IMAGE TO SMARTPHONE.
    ▪ Press RESET ORDER first to remove the "upload to smartphone" signal from every picture.

❖ **Select the pictures you want to upload:** After choosing which photos to upload, click MENU/OK.
  ▪ Press DISP/BACK before marking if you want to see only the photos that fit your criteria.
  ▪ To choose every photo, press the Q button.
  ▪ All photographs in between are selected when the AEL/AFL button is pressed on two pictures.

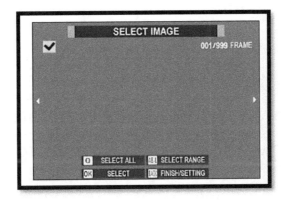

❖ Select "START TRANSFER" after pressing DISP/BACK.
  ▪ A few photos will be shared.

Filtering Images

To show just photos that fit certain requirements, select FILTERING by pressing DISP/BACK on the picture-selection dial.

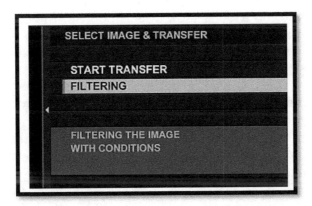

Selecting FILTERING will remove all postmarks. Requests for image transfers may include up to 999 images. You cannot select any of the following to upload.
❖ Protected images.
❖ Movies

❖ RAW pictures

❖ "Gift" photos, or images captured with other cameras

Uploads to the associated device will continue even when the camera is turned off if you select ON for both IMAGE TRANSFER WHILE POWER OFF and Bluetooth/SMARTPHONE SETTING > Bluetooth ON/OFF in the network/USB settings menu. You can access the picture-selection dialog by pressing the Fn1 button while SELECT & SMARTPHONE TRANSFER ORDER is selected for BUTTON/DIAL SETTING > Fn1 BUTTON SETTING.

Wireless communication

With the FUJIFILM Camera Remote app loaded, this setting allows you to connect your camera to smartphones and tablets. Both iOS and Android smartphones and tablets can use the software. Once connected, you may use your phone to see the camera's photos, download specific images, control the camera remotely, or provide the camera's position data so that your photos can be geotagged. Go to the SHOOTING SETTINGS menu as well to accomplish this. As mentioned before, the Wi-Fi or Fn button on every X Series camera is already configured to this setting. The WIRELESS COMMUNICATION option should be one of your buttons if you utilize the Camera Remote app. You can also add it to your MY MENU for convenient access. Therefore, when you've taken a great picture and are eager to share it, you don't need to search for this thing in the alternatives. You can connect to the smartphone by pressing the Fn1 button if you select WIRELESS COMMUNICATION under BUTTON/DIAL SETTING > Fn1 BUTTON SETTING.

SLIDE SHOW

Watch pictures in a slide show that plays automatically. Choose MENU/OK to get started. Push the focus stick (lever) to the right or left to move forward or backward. You can ring the program at any moment by pressing DISP/BACK to read on-screen assistance. By selecting OK/MENU, you can end the show at any moment. The camera won't shut off by itself if a slide show is playing.

PHOTOBOOK ASSIST

This feature is awesome. It enables you to create and present groupings of images that look like the pages of a small picture book or a stack of tiny prints. It's great that the images seem better even though they take up a little less screen real estate. Choose this option from the PLAYBACK MENU to create a PHOTOBOOK. To choose pictures for your book and a cover photo, select NEW BOOK, then look through your photos and follow the on-screen directions. One of the selections will be used as the main image if you don't select another one. (Books may contain up to 300 photos.) Once you're done, click OK to add the new book to your list. You can now read your book and return to the main menu. To remove the book or make modifications, press MENU/OK. Only BOOK 1, BOOK 2, BOOK 3, and so forth can be used to identify your photobooks. It is impossible to change their names. It would be a great touch to change the names. You can store copies of your bound photobooks on your computer if you have Fuji's MyFinePix Studio Software for Windows. Since I haven't used this program previously, I can't determine whether it's worth the money.

PHOTOBOOK VIEWING

Press MENU/OK to bring up the book, then choose a book from the book help menu and move the focus stick (photo lever) around the photos. Modifying and removing picture albums. Choose OK/MENU after displaying the photo book. After selecting your preferred option, adhere to the on-screen directions. The following alternatives will be shown.

❖ **EDIT:** Make the necessary changes to the book as described in "Creating a Photobook."

❖ **ERASE:** Discard the book.

PRINT ORDER (DPOF)

With this option, you can create a digital "print order" for DPOF-capable printers. However, printing requires DPOF. This technique allows you to store print-related data on your memory card, including which digital photos should be printed and in what quantity. Unfortunately, like many other technical trends, this one seems to have disappeared. The DPOF format is no longer widely used as the majority of printers are portable. If your printer has an SD card connector, you might still be able to use this feature. Select this item from the menu to start your PRINT ORDER. Next, decide if you want to add the recording date to your photos. You can start your order anew by pressing RESET ALL, then MENU or OK.

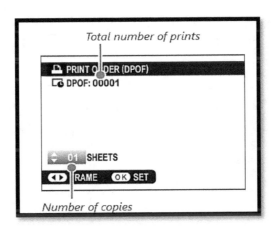

Now you may choose which pictures to print and in what quantities. Once you're done, press MENU/OK once more. All you need to do now is insert your memory card into a printer that supports DPOF and hit print. The printer will receive instructions on which image to print next from the PRINT ORDER information on the card. That's how easy it is.

INSTAX PRINTER PRINT

You may print straight from your camera if you have an INSTAX Share printer. Turn your INSTAX printer on to start the Wi-Fi connection. Then select this menu option on your camera.

Once a picture has been connected, you can print it by scrolling through your frames. Click OK to send it to the printer. The printing process starts as soon as you click OK, and your photo will be ready. Similar to magic. I truly value the INSTAX approach! The experience is great whether you print from your phone or your camera. The latest iteration of the INSTAX SHARE SP-2 printer enhances image quality and dynamic range. It's both familiar and exciting to have a photograph you took come to life in front of you as a print the size of a baseball card.

DISP ASPECT

This option allows you to select how HD devices with a 3:2 aspect ratio display photographs when you connect your camera to another device via HDMI. Select either 3:2 to show the entire image with black bars on either side or 16:9 to show the image with the top and bottom cropped off.

CHAPTER ELEVEN
UNDERSTANDING SOUND SETTING

Modify the camera's audio

Press [MENU/OK], pick the 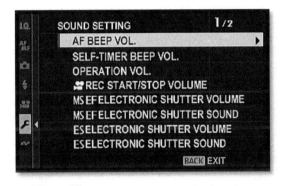 ([SET UP]) tab, and then select [SOUND SET-UP] to access the sound settings.

- ❖ [AF BEEP VOL.]
- ❖ [SELF-TIMER BEEP VOL.]
- ❖ [OPERATION VOL.]

- ❖ [REC START/STOP VOLUME]
- ❖ MS EF [ELECTRONIC SHUTTER VOLUME]
- ❖ MS EF [ELECTRONIC SHUTTER SOUND]
- ❖ ES [ELECTRONIC SHUTTER VOLUME]
- ❖ ES [ELECTRONIC SHUTTER SOUND]
- ❖ [PLAYBACK VOLUME]
- ❖ [4ch AUDIO PLAYBACK]

AF BEEP VOLUME

The camera beeps and the AF points you set turn green when the autofocus locks onto your subject. You can adjust the volume of this feature or disable it to stop it from beeping.

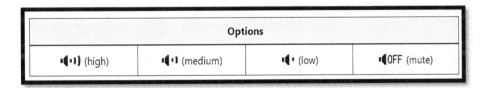

Options			
🔊 (high)	🔉 (medium)	🔈 (low)	🔇OFF (mute)

SELF-TIMER BEEP VOLUME

As previously mentioned, the Self-Timer needs the same supplies. You can select from three different sound levels or turn off the buzzer.

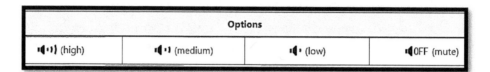

OPERATION VOLUME

This controls the sound level while navigating the menus. During the default selection process, you will hear "little clicks." The way you text on an iPhone with clicks enabled is comparable to this. You may turn off the clicks or select from three different sound levels. My cameras have all three of these settings off. I'll go crazy after a certain number of clicks and beeps.

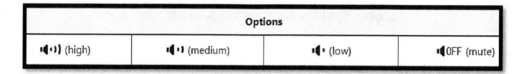

The REC START/STOP VOLUME

At the beginning and finish of the movie recording, adjust the volume.

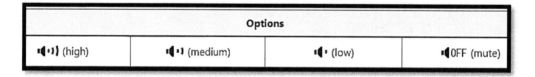

Headphones volume

When using headphones with the VPB-XT2 power booster grip, like when filming or watching videos, you can adjust the volume level. To turn off the sound, hit "OFF" or select a value between 1 and 10.

ELECTRONIC SHUTTER Volume

This controls how loud your electronic silencer is. You may add a fake "shutter sound" to make the ES sound more realistic—or at least louder—because it doesn't create noise on its own. To make your ES quiet, you may also turn off all of the audio. This is the choice for you if you're taking pictures in a private setting and don't want anyone to know, or if you're shooting in a theater or on a movie set.

ELECTRONIC SHUTTER SOUND

Your electric shutter has three different sound settings.

❖ Sound 1 has a slight "tick."

❖ SOUND 2 creates a richer "chick" sound akin to an old Roland drum machine handclap.

❖ Sound 3 makes a brief "ca-chick!" sound at 1/1,000 seconds, which is similar to a shutter ring. It's kind of adorable.

I've used number one, but I like number two. Three was the most you could select.

Playback volume

Modify the audio playing volume for voice annotations and videos.

Options										
[0]	[1]	[2]	[3]	[4]	[5]	[6]	[7]	[8]	[9]	[10]

About 4ch Audio Playback

To watch a 4ch movie, change the audio settings.

❖ **XLR:** The XLR microphone adapter plays recorded audio from external microphones connected to the camera.

❖ **CAMERA:** Sound recordings made by the camera's built-in microphone or additional microphones attached to the microphone jack may be played.

Note: Clicking the middle of the focus stick (also known as the focus lever) allows you to change sources while watching the playback display.

CHAPTER TWELVE

ABOUT SCREEN SETTING

Modify the display settings

Press [MENU/OK], pick the 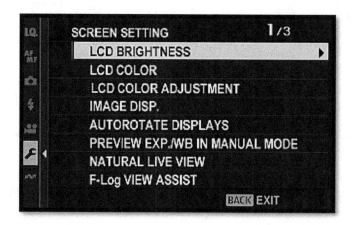 ([SET UP]) tab, and then select [SCREEN SET-UP] to access display settings.

- ❖ [LCD BRIGHTNESS]
- ❖ [LCD COLOR]
- ❖ [LCD COLOR ADJUSTMENT]
- ❖ [IMAGE DISP.]
- ❖ [AUTOROTATE DISPLAYS]
- ❖ [PREVIEW EXP./WB IN MANUAL MODE]
- ❖ [NATURAL LIVE VIEW]
- ❖ [F-Log VIEW ASSIST]
- ❖ [ELECTRONIC LEVEL SETTING]
- ❖ [FRAMING GUIDELINE]
- ❖ [AUTOROTATE PB]
- ❖ [FOCUS SCALE UNITS]
- ❖ [APERTURE UNIT FOR CINEMA LENS]
- ❖ [DISP. CUSTOM SETTING]
- ❖ [LARGE INDICATORS MODE(LCD)]
- ❖ [LARGE INDICATORS DISP. SETTING]
- ❖ [INFORMATION CONTRAST ADJ.]
- ❖ [LOCATION INFO]

- ❖   [Q MENU BACKGROUND]

❖  [Q MENU BACKGROUND]

View Mode Settings

You can adjust the LCD panel view modes, EVF/OVF (electronic/optical viewfinder), and eye sensor settings.

❖ **AUTO:** Depending on the surrounding lighting, the camera automatically sets the brightness to a predetermined level.

❖ **MANUAL:** Manually change the brightness from -7 to +5.

EVF Color

This changes the color of the LCD on your computer. In essence, it modifies the intensity a little. I never changed this setting, and it's always on.

EVF Color Modification

It is possible to alter the color of the electronic LCD display.

❖ Use the focus stick (handle) to change colors.

❖ Select either "OK" or "MENU."

The brightness of the LCD

EVF Brightness is comparable to the above, but for the LCD screen.

Modify the monitor brightness

Options										
[-5]	[-4]	[-3]	[-2]	[-1]	[0]	[+1]	[+2]	[+3]	[+4]	[+5]

LCD Color

EFF Color, just like before, but with an LCD screen. Once again, I have never changed this. I think the LCD screen looks amazing.

Modify the saturation of the monitor

Options										
[-5]	[-4]	[-3]	[-2]	[-1]	[0]	[+1]	[+2]	[+3]	[+4]	[+5]

LCD COLOR ADJUSTMENT

The LCD monitor's display color can be altered.
- ❖ To switch colors, use the focus stick (lever).
- ❖ Select either "OK" or "MENU."

IMAGE DISPLAY

This feature allows you to define how long photographs are exhibited after they have been recorded.
- ❖ The LCD/EVF displays photos in CONTINUOUS mode until you activate the MENU/OK or shutter buttons. Remember that you may zoom in to 100% while viewing photographs by using the back command dial.
- ❖ To display images for the desired duration or until you push the shutter again, choose 1.5 SEC or 0.5 SEC.
- ❖ **OFF:** The camera does not show the picture after it has been taken.

Mine are always off. I don't have to go through each frame I take. It also saves battery life.

AUTOROTATE DISPLAYS

When this option is enabled, tilting the camera will cause the shooting information and other indications to move to their correct positions. I always have this option enabled.

PREVIEW EXPOSURE/WHITE BALANCE IN MANUAL MODE

The exciting part is about to begin! To test exposure and white balance settings and make adjustments when shooting in manual exposure mode, select PREVIEW EXP/WB IN MANUAL MODE. The majority of the time, you want the camera to operate in this default mode. Remember that one benefit of using a mirrorless camera is that the LCD and EVF capture the image directly from the sensor, allowing you to observe exposure changes as they occur. To put it another way, the picture displayed on the LCD is exactly what you will see when you take a picture. Generally speaking, you should look at this information because it eliminates any uncertainty over the quality of your photograph, particularly when you're shooting in low light. Your Fuji will act more like a DSLR if you turn this setting off; therefore the picture you see might not be the one you got. Unless you like the intrigue of challenging exposures, you should leave this at PREVIEW EXP/WB.

At what point would you like to disable this setting?

Yes, while photographing with a flash. Du ring the ambient exposure setting can occasionally be too dark to view on the LCD. You're using the flash to provide illumination while filming an event in total darkness. You have the exposure set to about 1/250 seconds. In a dark setting, f/8 will make it too dark to see anything on the LCD. The view in your EVF or LCD will remain bright and normal regardless of exposure if you disable this setting. This helps you see and write about your topic more clearly. You can PREVIEW WB only in this case. This will give you a preview of the LCD's white balance, but not its exposure. This can be the greatest choice when photographing with several lights of different color temperatures. Or, if you're shooting in RAW and plan to adjust the WB settings on your computer afterwards. If you frequently use a flash, assign this function to an Fn button for convenient access or add it to your MY MENU.

NATURAL LIVE VIEW

You can choose whether the monitor shows the effects of white balance, film emulation, and other parameters.

- ❖ **ON:** Improves shadow visibility in backlit, low contrast, and hard-to-see subjects as compared to camera settings that are not visible on the screen. Compared to the final image, the colors and tones will be different. To highlight the impact of sepia and monochrome displays, the display settings will be altered.
- ❖ While the display is off, test the white balance, film emulation, and other settings.

F-Log View Assist

When recording or viewing F-log videos, choose ON to provide a tone-corrected preview view (BT.709).

ELECTRONIC LEVEL SETTING

Using the virtual horizon display, adjust the parameters for usage when taking pictures.

FRAMING GUIDELINE

Select a shooting mode frame grid.

Option	Description	Display
⊞ GRID 9	For "rule of thirds" composition.	🖼
⊞ GRID 24	A six-by-four grid.	🖼
▣ HD FRAMING	Frame HD pictures in the crop shown by the lines at the top and bottom of the display.	🖼

AUTOROTATE PB

Activate the feature that rotates "tall" (portrait-oriented) images automatically while they are being played.

FOCUS SCALE UNITS

Select the focus distance indication's units.

Aperture Unit for Cinema Lens

You can select whether the aperture is shown as an f/number (for still camera lenses) or a T-number (for movie camera lenses) when a FUJINON MKX-series lens is attached. Instructions for using cinema lenses are included in the material that comes with the lens.

- ❖ T NUMBER: To measure lens aperture, cinematographers frequently utilize T numbers. Exposure estimations are optimized by lens transmittance.
- ❖ F NUMBER: To calculate lens aperture, photographers frequently utilize the F number. Since lens transmittance is taken to be 100%, different exposures may be obtained from the same aperture depending on the lens.

DISP. CUSTOM SETTING

Select the objects displayed in the shooting display.

LARGE INDICATOR MODE (EVF)

To show large signs in the optical or electronic viewfinder, select ON. By selecting SCREEN SET-UP > LARGE indications DISPLAY SETTINGS, you can change the indications that are shown.

- ❖ Some icons are hidden when LARGE INDICATORS MODE (EVF) is selected as ON.
- ❖ To activate and deactivate the LARGE INDICATORS MODE, press the function button connected to it.

LARGE INDICATORS MODE (LCD)

To show large signs on the LCD monitor, select ON. By selecting SCREEN SET-UP > LARGE indications DISPLAY SETTINGS, you can change the indications that are shown.

❖ Some icons are hidden when the LARGE INDICATORS MODE (LCD) option is selected.

❖ To activate and deactivate the LARGE INDICATORS MODE, press the function button connected to it.

LARGE INDICATOR DISPLAY SETTING

From SCREEN SET-UP > LARGE indications MODE (EVF/OVF) or LARGE INDICATORS MODE (LCD), select the indications that will be shown when ON is selected.

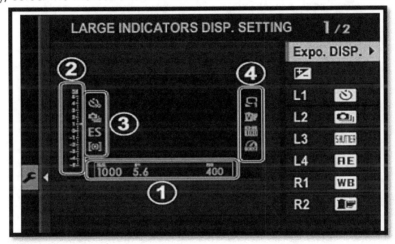

❖ **Expo. DISP.:** Choose items from the bottom-of-the-display. The items that have been selected are shown by the checkmarks. Select an item, and then click MENU/OK to deselect it.

❖ **Scale:** Click ON to bring up the exposure monitor.

❖ Select up to four enormous icons (L1, L2, L3, and L4) to appear on the left side of the screen.

❖ Select the R1, R2, R3, and R4 large icons to display on the right side of the screen.

CHAPTER THIRTEEN
ABOUT BUTTON/DIAL SETTING

Explore camera control options

Choose [BUTTON/DIAL SETTING], choose the  ([SET UP]) tab, then press [MENU/OK] to access control options.

❖ FOCUS LEVER SETTING

❖ 📷 EDIT/SAVE QUICK MENU

❖ 🎥 EDIT/SAVE QUICK MENU

❖ FUNCTION (Fn) SETTING

❖ POWER ZOOM LENS FUNCTION (Fn) SETTING

❖ COMMAND DIAL SETTING

❖ 🎛 S.S. OPERATION

❖ COMMAND DIAL DIRECTION

❖ SHUTTER AF

❖ SHUTTER AE

❖ SHOOT WITHOUT LENS

❖ SHOOT WITHOUT CARD

❖ LENS ZOOM/FOCUS SETTING

❖ AE/AF-LOCK MODE

❖ AWB-LOCK MODE

❖ APERTURE RING SETTING (A)

❖ APERTURE RING

❖ ▶ REC BUTTON SETTING

❖ TOUCH SCREEN SETTING

❖ LOCK

FOCUS LEVER SETTING

You might lock the focus button joystick when using this feature. Lock the stick after holding it down for about two seconds to bring up the menu display. Press the LOCK (OFF) button to stop the joystick from completing concentration tasks. You won't be able to move or select your focus points once you have this set. Your current focus point will stay exactly where you left it when you lock the handle. You may still navigate through your photos and select different options by using the lever. Press and hold once more, then select ON to unlock. (It is also opened by the choice in the middle.) You can now get back to work. For whatever reason, the focus lever has stopped if it does not move or allow you to select focus points. Just press and hold to bring up the unlock option once more. Select the functions by pressing the focus stick's center (also known as the focus lever) or by pressing the stick's left, right, up, or down.

❖ PUSH

Option	Description
[OFF]	Pressing the center of the stick has no effect.
[EDIT FOCUS AREA]	Press the center of the stick to choose the focus area size. If [😊][FACE/EYE DETECTION SETTING] or [SUBJECT DETECTION SETTING] is on, you can instead position the focus frame over the desired face, eye, animal, or object.
[ZOOM]	Press the center of the stick to zoom in on the active focus area
[RESET TO CENTER]	Press the center of the stick to select the center focus area.

❖ TILT ☼

Option	Description
[OFF]	Pressing the stick up, down, left, or right has no effect.
[DIRECT AF POINT SELECTION]	Choose the focus area without leaving the shooting display.
[EDIT FOCUS AREA]	Press the stick up, down, left, or right to view a focus-area display and choose the focus area.

Edit/Save Quick Menu

This is the official menu item that lets you change your Q menu. Yes, you know that pressing and holding the Q button will cause it to ring there faster. To modify your Q menu, you shouldn't ever need to access the BUTTON/DIAL SETTING menu.

FN/AE-L/AF-L BUTTON SETTING

You can personalize all of your Fn, AE-L, and AF-L buttons with this menu item. Anyway, I don't want to see you in this dark area of the camera menu again because you know a quicker way to configure your Fn buttons. Press and hold the DISP/BACK buttons instead.

❖ Holding the shutter button halfway to focus is no longer necessary when AF-ON is connected to a button. You may simply push the button.
❖ Click the MODELING FLASH button to test the flash.
❖ To limit flash output according to the FLASH SETTING you select, press the TTL-LOCK button.

COMMAND DIAL SETTING

This menu allows you to change the way your command dials work. It may be adjusted such that the front dial controls the aperture and the back dial controls the shutter speed. As an alternative, the aperture can be controlled by the rear dial and the shutter speed by the front dial. You could decide to do so. Anything that makes you feel at home or at ease. You may already have a solution in place if you recently switched from a Nikon or Canon system. Therefore, you might want to set up your Fuji the same way you usually do in order to facilitate the transition as much as possible.

❖ Press and hold the front command dial's center to bring up the Command Dial Settings.
❖ Press the center of the front command dial in the following order to switch between settings: FRONT COMMAND DIAL 1, FRONT COMMAND DIAL 2, FRONT COMMAND DIAL 3, and FRONT COMMAND DIAL 4.

The SS Operation

To change your settings when shooting in Program mode, use the shutter speed slider. Assume, for instance, that you are in Program mode and observe a scenario in progress. It could be your energetic kids or grandkids playing with a dog, or it could be a bald eagle in flight. You can see that the shutter speed and aperture are set to 1/320 sec. at f/5.6 if you raise the camera to your eye. 1/320 seconds might not be enough to halt the activity, particularly if you're using a long lens that requires a higher shutter speed to capture sharp images. Now that this option is active, you may quickly adjust the shutter speed using the command dial you've configured to find a better setting, such 1/1250 seconds at f/2.8. There's no doubt the bird will freeze. (SS on the back dial is what I like best.) Keep in mind that the shutter speeds you can use in Program mode are restricted by the ISO setting you are using at the moment and the amount of available light. The possible shutter speeds are limited, but they will provide adequate exposure. It's also possible to remove this setting, though I'm not sure why. You ought to keep it on, in my opinion.

COMMAND DIAL DIRECTION

By turning the command dials in the proper way, you can alter the numbers. The command dials on the front and back can be adjusted separately.

❖ Turn the dial to the right to obtain greater numbers or move on to the next item.
❖ Turn the dial to the left to see higher numbers or move on to the next item.

SHUTTER AF/Shutter AE

This setting has been greatly enhanced by several recent software updates, making it an even more alluring option. Usually, the camera automatically focuses and locks in the exposure when you press the shutter halfway down. You can split one or both of these responsibilities using the SHUTTER AF/AE settings. Additionally, you can configure the camera to function differently in AF-S and AF-C modes. To be clear, in AF-S mode, the camera locks focus when the shutter button is partially depressed. As long as you hold down the button, it will stay in this position. The focus is continuously changing in AF-C mode when the shutter button is halfway pushed.

Shutter AF

With this setting, you can select different settings for AF-S and AF-C, turn both off and end focusing with the shutter button, or leave one or both on by default. Pressing the shutter in AF-S mode will focus and lock the image if you have AF-S enabled and AF-C disabled. Pressing the shutter in AF-C mode will not focus the image.

Shutter AE

Similar to SHUTTER AF, SHUTTER AE lets you change the operating parameters that determine when and how the camera locks exposure in AF-S/MF or AF-C mode. When the shutter button is partially depressed, either setting instructs the camera to lock exposure. Even if you just push the shutter halfway, the camera will still adjust the exposure if you switch off one or both of them.

Here's why I think real-world shooting could benefit from this choice. Assume that, as in the picture above, you and I are photographing a group of cyclists racing across a light and dark area. Maybe we are in the Serengeti shooting a group of zebras. As you can see, in order to keep the moving subjects in focus, we are both utilizing AF-C and Continuous mode. I leave AF-C on when using SHUTTER AF since I don't enjoy having to press the back button to focus. All of the subjects you have chosen for the photo session are in the sun. As they pass through the area, I shoot them in the interim. (You seem to be more in charge of what you shoot than I am! You keep AF-C off when using SHUTTER AE because it eliminates the need to adjust exposure in one type of light before shooting in another. I switched off AF-C in SHUTTER AE mode, though, because I don't want my exposure to lock on a sunny spot right before I take a burst when they ride their bikes from the sun to the shade. Better outcomes are achieved because these options enable each of us to adjust our X-M5 to best suit our own shooting preferences.

SHOOT WITHOUT LENS

When no lens is mounted, select ON to enable the shutter release.

SHOOT WITHOUT CARD

To try out a different lens, camera, or setting, you don't necessarily need a memory card in your camera. (I'll say it again: make sure your camera has a memory card.) This feature allows you to turn off the shutter if you are not carrying a card. The shutter is locked when it is set to OFF.

LENSZOOM/FOCUS SETTING

For compatible lenses with power zoom or focus rings, change the settings.

FOCUS RING ROTATE

This feature allows you to focus your camera in either clockwise or counterclockwise directions from close to a distance. If you are unable to adapt to the Fuji cameras' way of operation because you are used to a different camera system with focus rings that revolve in the opposite direction, this can be helpful. Mine is still in the same spot.

FOCUS RING OPERATION

The focus ring can be adjusted to control the camera's focus changes.
   ❖ NONLINEAR: Ring speed affects the concentration.
   ❖ LINEAR: By rotating the ring, the focus is changed linearly while maintaining a steady speed.

MF CONSTANT SPEED FOCUS (Fn)

With compatible power zoom lenses, you can adjust the speed at which the focus distance changes by pressing function buttons while manual focusing. The greater the number, the greater the rate.

CONSTANT SPEED ZOOM (Fn)

To adjust how quickly compatible power zoom lenses can be zoomed in or out, use the function buttons. The greater the number, the greater the rate.

CONSTANT SPEED ZOOM/FOCUS (Fn) OPERATION

Choose whether power focus or zoom must be started and stopped by pressing the function buttons on compatible power zoom lenses only once.
   - ❖ START/STOP SWITCH: Pressing the button once initiates the action, and pressing it again ends it.
   - ❖ ACTIVE WHEN PRESSING: When the button is pressed, the action continues, and when it is released, it stops.

ZOOM RING ROTATE

For compatible power zoom lenses, you can decide whether to reverse the zoom ring's rotation.

Ring for Zoom/Focus Control

On compatible power zoom lenses, choose the zoom/focus control ring's function.

AE/AF-LOCK MODE

It's a great place, but I doubt many people know about it. For this to work, keep in mind that your AE-L and AF-L keys need to be set to AE LOCK ONLY and AF LOCK ONLY, respectively. Pressing the AE-L or AF-L button will lock your exposure and/or focus for as long as you hold it down if the AE & AF ON WHEN pressed function is enabled.

AE and AF ON/OFF However, SWITCH means that if you hit the AE-L or AF-L button, the exposure and/or focus will be locked until you push the button again. I think SWITCH mode is a helpful function. The AE LOCK ONLY control can be configured to be an Fn button. After then, you might measure your topic. Once you've achieved a good exposure, you could release your finger from the button and press AE-L to lock in the exposure. Then, without the stress of exposure, which would be locked in and out of your control, you could establish the scene, focus, and pay attention. The shutter stays locked no matter how many times you press it. As long as your light doesn't change, you're fine. To see a new reading on the meter when the light changes, press the button once more. You're ready to go.

When photographing a motionless subject, the light may move. To accomplish the same goal, you might use AF-L in place of AE-L. While shooting, monitor the exposure and press to lock in the focus. With the exception of having to keep your finger down the entire time, the PRESSING mode is identical. This is one of those situations where your decisions determine everything. Find out if this is a good option for you and how it operates.

AWB-LOCK MODE

Ascertain the proper operation of the feature buttons that are configured for auto white balance (AWB) lock. The auto white balance lock will preserve the white balance value that the camera provides if you select AUTO for white balance.
- ❖ Press the AWB ON WHEN PRESSING button to lock the auto white balance.
- ❖ Press the AWB ON/OFF SWITCH button once to lock the auto white balance. Just push the button again to unlock it.

APERTURE SETTING

The majority of Fuji lenses have aperture rings, but they are not always present. Follow these instructions to adjust the aperture if your lens lacks a ring. It can be difficult to use in all shooting modes, as I know from owning the small pancake 27 mm f/2.8 lenses. RED/BLUE televisions may have this option in one of their RED MENUS.

- ❖ To change the aperture, use the front command dial (AUTO + MANUAL mode). To select A (Auto aperture), turn the lens past your lowest aperture (the highest number).
- ❖ **AUTO:** The aperture is chosen by the camera on its own. With this setting, the camera can only be used in the P (Program) and S (Shutter Priority) modes.
- ❖ The front command dial can be used to manually change the aperture. The camera will only use the A (Aperture Priority) and M (Manual Exposure) exposure modes when you select this option.

FN1 BUTTON SETTING

During playback, select the function of the Fn1 button
- ❖ The current photo is chosen for transfer by pressing the SMARTPHONE TRANSFER ORDER button. The Bluetooth/SMARTPHONE SETTINGS choices will appear if the camera is not currently linked to a smartphone.
- ❖ Press the SELECT & SMARTPHONE TRANSFER ORDER button, which displays a screen, to move photos to a smartphone. The Bluetooth/SMARTPHONE SETTINGS choices will show up if the camera is not already linked to a smartphone.
- ❖ The current photo is transferred to Frame.io by clicking the Frame.io TRANSFER ORDER button.
- ❖ Press the button to establish a wireless connection.

TOUCH SCREEN SETTING

Turn touch-screen controls on or off.

SCREEN TOUCH SETTING

- ❖ **ON:** When filming, the LCD panel can be used as a touch screen. OFF: The touch controls are not in use.

DOUBLE-TAP SETTING

- ❖ **ON:** To focus on your topic while shooting, tap the LCD screen twice.
- ❖ **OFF:** Touch zoom is not active.

Touch Function

- ❖ **ON:** Turn on the touches feature.
- ❖ **OFF:** Disable touch sensitivity.

Settings for the Touch Screen

- ❖ **ON:** During playing, use the LCD screen as a touch screen.
- ❖ **OFF:** The touch buttons are not in use.

FUNCTION SELECTION

Select the controls to be locked when you select SELECTED FUNCTION for LOCK SETTING. By pressing and holding MENU/OK, the controls associated with the specified FUNCTION can be locked at any point during shooting. Press and hold the button one more to unlock the controls.

CHAPTER FOURTEEN
THE POWER MANAGEMENT

Modify the power management configuration

Press [MENU/OK], pick the 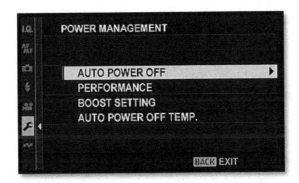 ([SET UP]) tab, and then select [POWER MANAGEMENT] to access the power management settings.

* [AUTO POWER OFF]
* [PERFORMANCE]
* [BOOST SETTING]
* [AUTO POWER OFF TEMP.]

AUTO POWER-OFF

Longer battery life can be achieved by programming the camera to shut off after a predetermined period of time. 15 seconds, 30 seconds, one minute, two minutes, or five minutes are the options available to you. After selecting "OFF," the camera will continue to operate until you manually switch it off. Or as long as the battery is in good condition.

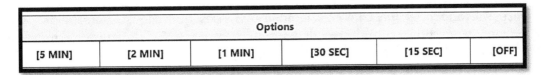

Options					
[5 MIN]	[2 MIN]	[1 MIN]	[30 SEC]	[15 SEC]	[OFF]

PERFORMANCE

This camera's performance (PERFORMANCE) function is intended to provide optimal performance. The camera features normal AF speed, display quality, and an LCD refresh rate of 60 frames per second when it is in its default NORMAL setting. The AF speed is lowered from 0.08 to 0.06 seconds in the new BOOST mode, however the LCD update rate increases to 100 frames per second and the display quality is enhanced. Get more out of BOOST mode with the Vertical Power Booster Grip. By enabling you to utilize three batteries simultaneously—two in the grip and one in the camera body—BOOST mode with the grip improves the performance of the X-M5.

Along with the following efficiency gains, the AF speed and EVF were improved:

❖ The shutter time lag is between 0.05 and 0.045 seconds; the shutter interval was lowered from 0.19 to 0.17 seconds.

❖ There was a decrease in the interval between blackouts from 130 to 114 msec.

❖ The continuous shooting rate is increased from 8 to 11 frames per second by the electronic shutter.

In addition, the grip features the Q menu, AE-L, AF-L, and FOCUS ASSIST buttons, a focus handle, a vertical shutter button, two command dials, and a focus assist button. Especially with a longer lens, this grip makes it easy to shoot vertically. Additionally, it features a 9-volt wall charger that takes about two hours to fully charge two batteries. There is a headphone jack on the grip as well. What is meant by all of this? When using the vertical grip, it shows that the camera is reasonably stable. The 50-140mm and XF 100-400mm lenses work well together to capture a variety of scenes, including animals and fast-moving objects. It has also extended the life of my battery when I'm filming. Although I don't use it much, I'm happy to have it on hand in case I need it. Yes, even if BOOST mode lets you use two extra batteries, it wastes a lot of power and the grip makes it heavier and bulkier. Nevertheless, the grip is excellent. As mentioned before, you need to gain a handle on motion, sports, and video photography.

Adjust EVF/LCD boost

Setting PERFORMANCE to BOOST may cause the LCD viewer and EVF to behave differently.

❖ In order to improve subject visibility in low light conditions, EVF/LCD LOW LIGHT PRIORITY modifies display brightness. Ghosting can be caused by motion blur.

❖ Give EVF/LCD resolution top priority to enhance screen clarity and detail visibility.

❖ To enhance motion smoothness, the EVF frame rate (100P) was prioritized.

AUTO POWER-OFF TEMP

A notice will appear if the camera's temperature rises above a set threshold. It will immediately stop shooting and shut down if the temperature rises more. Choose the temperature at which the camera will automatically switch off.

❖ **STANDARD:** The camera automatically turns off when it reaches the STANDARD temperature.

❖ **HIGH:** Continuous shooting is made possible by high temperatures. Customers now have more time to record movies and engage in other activities. This option should only be used after the camera has been put on a stand or other precautions have been taken to prevent the user from standing close to the camera for an extended amount of time, as remaining close to the camera at these high temperatures could cause low-temperature burns.

CHAPTER FIFTEEN

MODIFY THE FILE MANAGEMENT CONFIGURATION

Press [MENU/OK], pick the ▢ ([SET UP]) tab, and then select [SAVE DATA SET-UP] to open the file management options.

- ❖ [FRAME NO.]
- ❖ [EDIT FILE NAME]
- ❖ [SELECT FOLDER]
- ❖ [COPYRIGHT INFO]
- ❖ [GEOTAGGING]

THE FRAME NUMBER

A four-digit file number that is obtained by appending one to the most recent file number used is used to name new images. As shown, the file number appears when the video is playing. FRAME NO. Indicates if the current memory card is formatted or if file numbering is reset to 0001 upon inserting a new memory card.

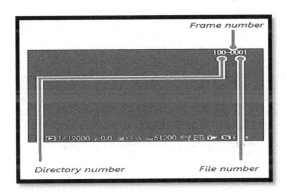

❖ **CONTINUOUS:** The highest or most recent number is used to begin continuous file numbering. To reduce the number of photos with duplicate file names, choose this option.

❖ **RENEW:** The numbering will return to 0001 following formatting or the insertion of a fresh memory card.

The shutter release will not function if the frame number is 999 or higher. Turn off the camera and put in a formatted memory card before you start shooting again. The file number doesn't change when you select CONTINUOUS under USER SETTINGS > RESET, FRAME NO. Photographs taken with different cameras may have different frame counts.

EDIT FILE NAME

Images from Fuji cameras are given distinct file name prefixes based on whether they were taken in Adobe RGB or sRGB color mode. Whereas sRGB begins with four letters, Adobe RGB begins with a three-letter prefix followed by an underscore.

❖ sRGB prefix: DSCF

❖ DSF is the Adobe RGB prefix

The underscore cannot be removed; however you can alter the default start to any letter or number. **For instance, you can modify it to generate unique file names for your image files:**

❖ sRGB: DANB0001.

❖ Adobe ID: DHB0001.

Using your own file names is what I advise. You can quickly recognize your own photos or images taken with various cameras thanks to it. For instance, you may create suffixes that represent a nation or a year. There are a number of options. Consider the possibilities. I hear your tiny wheels whirling already.

SELECT FOLDER

You can choose the folder to utilize for storing future photos after creating groups.

Option	Description
[SELECT FOLDER]	To choose the folder in which subsequent pictures will be stored, press the focus stick (focus lever) up or down to highlight an existing folder and press **[MENU/OK]**.
[CREATE FOLDER]	Enter a five-character folder name. The new folder will be created with the next picture you take and subsequent pictures will be stored in that folder.

COPYRIGHT INFO

New photos can have copyright information added to them as they are taken by using exif tags. Only photos taken after updates show that the copyright information has changed.

Option	Description
[DISP COPYRIGHT INFO]	View the current copyright information.
[ENTER AUTHOR'S INFO]	Enter the creator's name.
[ENTER COPYRIGHT INFO]	Enter the name of the copyright holder.
[DELETE COPYRIGHT INFO]	Delete the current copyright information. This change applies only to images taken after this option is selected; copyright information recorded with existing images is not affected.

GEOTAGGING

If ON is selected, location information that has been downloaded from a smartphone will be integrated into photos as they are being taken.

Options	
[ON]	[OFF]

179

CHAPTER SIXTEEN

UNDERSTANDING CONNECTIONS

Making a Wi-Fi Network Connection

To download pictures or control the camera while viewing them via the lens on the phone's photo display, pair the camera with a smartphone over Bluetooth. The camera instantly establishes a wireless local area network (LAN) when you transfer photos to your phone.

> - Installing smartphone apps.
> - Connect to a smartphone.
> - Use the Smartphone App

Installing Smartphone Applications

Before you may link the camera to your phone, you must install at least one app designed specifically for smartphones. This website allows you to download the apps you want to have on your phone. Which applications are available depends on the smartphone's operating system.

Connecting to a smartphone

Make a Bluetooth connection between your phone and camera.
   ❖ Press the Bluetooth button when the camera is in shooting mode.

   ▪   To move on to Step 3, hold down the DISP/BACK button while the video is playing.
   ❖ Select "Bluetooth" and then "OK" or "MENU."

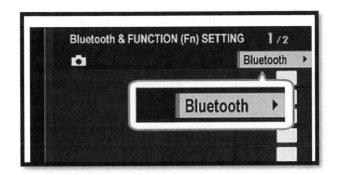

❖ Select MENU/OK after selecting PAIRING.

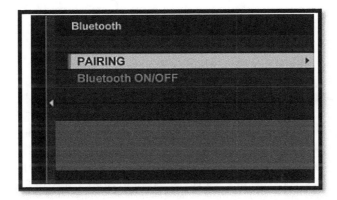

❖ Connect your phone to the camera and launch the app: The phone and camera will immediately pair via Bluetooth after the setup is finished. The camera's screen will display a white Bluetooth symbol and a smartphone icon once a connection has been made.

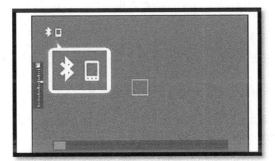

- When the app is used, the camera will connect to the phone after pairing.
- Longer battery life is achieved by turning off Bluetooth when a smartphone's camera is not connected.

Utilizing a USB cable to connect to a smartphone

You can use a USB connection to link your smartphone and camera with the FUJIFILM XApp. iOS 15.2 or later is required if you own an iOS smartphone.
- ❖ Select "POWER SUPPLY OFF/COMM ON" from the network/USB settings menu.
- ❖ Select the CONNECTION MODE USB card reader.
- ❖ Open the FUJIFILM XApp on your mobile device.
- ❖ Switch on the camera and use a USB cable to connect it to the smartphone.

Using the Smartphone Application

Go to Bluetooth/SMARTPHONE SETTINGS > Bluetooth ON/OFF and choose ON before continuing.

Choosing and Obtaining Images through the Mobile App

You can save specific photos on your phone by using the app.

Uploading Images as They're Captured

Any images you take will be instantly sent to the device you are connected to if you choose ON for Bluetooth/SMARTPHONE SETTING > AUTO IMAGE TRANSFER ORDER in the network/USB settings menu. If ON is chosen in both IMAGE TRANSFER WHILE POWER OFF and Bluetooth/SMARTPHONE SETTING > Bluetooth ON/OFF in the network/USB settings menu, uploading to a paired device will proceed even if the camera is off. To reduce the size of files when they are uploaded, choose "ON" for Bluetooth/SMARTPHONE setup > RESIZE IMAGE FOR SMARTPHONE in the network/USB configuration menu. The network/USB settings menu (Bluetooth/SMARTPHONE SETTING > SELECT FILE TYPE) allows you to select the format in which images are delivered.

Choosing Images in the Playback Menu to Upload

Go to TRANSFER IMAGE TO SMARTPHONE > SELECT IMAGE & TRANSFER to select which photographs to send via Bluetooth to a connected phone or tablet.

Using USB to connect to smartphones

It lets you upload pictures and connects to PCs and phones via USB.
- ▪ Transferring images to a mobile device.
- ▪ Attaching the camera to the computer.

Copying Images to a Smartphone

Choose AUTO or POWER SUPPLY OFF/COMM ON under USB POWER SUPPLY/COMM setup in the network/USB configuration menu before connecting to the smartphone to upload photos over USB.

For Customers Having Android Devices

* ❖ In the network/USB setting menu, choose AUTO or POWER SUPPLY OFF/COMM ON under USB POWER SUPPLY/COMM SETTING.
* ❖ Select the CONNECTION MODE USB card reader.
* ❖ Use a USB cord to link the smartphone and camera.
* ▪ Press "Cancel" to move on to the next step if the smartphone requests authorization for an app other than "Camera Importer" to access the camera.
* ❖ Click the "Connected to USB PTP" notification on your smartphone.
* ❖ Select "Camera Importer" from the list of recommended applications.

You may load photos and videos into your smartphone with the software, which will start up promptly. Please restart the app from step 3 if the message "There is no MTP device connected" appears. It's possible that some file types cannot be imported.

For customers that use iOS

* ❖ Select "POWER SUPPLY OFF/COMM ON" from the network/USB settings menu.
* ❖ Select the CONNECTION MODE USB card reader.
* ❖ Use a USB cord to link the smartphone and camera.

Use the photos app on your smartphone to import photos and videos.

Connecting Camera and Computer

* ❖ From the network/USB settings menu, select AUTO or POWER SUPPLY OFF/COMM ON for the USB POWER SUPPLY/COMM SETTING.
* ❖ Select the CONNECTION MODE USB card reader.
* ❖ Turn on the camera after connecting it to your PC via USB.
* ❖ Transfer images to your PC.
    * ▪ To copy images to your computer on Mac OS X and macOS, use Image Capture or similar software. To copy files larger than 4 GB, use a card reader.
    * ▪ **Windows:** To transfer images to your computer, use the operating system's applications.

Keep in mind: Before disconnecting the camera, turn it off.

* ▪ Verify that USB wires are plugged in and oriented correctly. Don't use a USB hub or keyboard to connect the camera to your PC.
* ▪ Power outages during a transfer could cause memory card damage or data loss. Make sure the battery is new or fully charged before connecting the camera.

- Importing or saving photographs may be prohibited when using a memory card with a large quantity of images. The program may not start up immediately. To move pictures, use a memory card reader.
- Verify that the front light is off or light green before shutting off the camera.
- When moving, don't unplug the USB cord. You risk losing data or damaging the memory card if you don't take this step.
- Before inserting or removing memory cards, unplug the camera.
- Unlike on a single computer, the program may not always allow you to view photographs saved on a network server.
- Until the copying message shows on the screen, do not unplug the USB cable or take the camera out of the computer. After the message is sent, data transfer might continue if a sizable number of photos are copied.
- Internet users are liable for any costs levied by their service provider or Phone Company.

Using Camera as a Webcam

The camera can be used as a webcam by connecting it to your computer.
- ❖ From the network/USB settings menu, choose AUTO or POWER SUPPLY OFF/COMM ON to modify the USB power supply/communication settings.
- ❖ The USB WEBCAM option is located in CONNECTION MODE.
- ❖ Use a USB cord to connect the camera to the computer. Next, switch the camera on.
- ❖ Decide which camera will be used to capture your video.

SHARE Printers for Instax

Using an Instax SHARE printer, print pictures from your digital camera.
- ❖ Creating a relationship.
- ❖ Producing images.

Setting up a Connection

From the network/USB settings menu, select instax PRINTER CONNECTION SETTING. Next, enter your password and the Instax SHARE printer's name (SSID).

The password and printer name (SSID)

The printer's name (SSID) and password (111) are visible around the base. Use the additional password you previously provided if you wish to print from your phone.

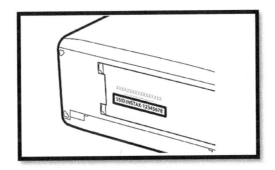

Printing Images

❖ Turn the printer on.

❖ Select instax PRINTER PRINT from the PLAY BACK MENU, which will enable the printer to connect to the camera.

❖ Choose MENU/OK after displaying the image you wish to print using the focus stick (focus button).

▪ The print area is less than the LCD screen;

▪ The display may vary depending on the printer; • No photos from other cameras may be printed.

185

❖ After supplying the printer with the photo, printing will start.

RAW Processing

X RAW STUDIO allows you to use the camera's image processing engine when editing RAW photos on your PC.

❖ From the network/USB settings menu, choose AUTO or POWER SUPPLY OFF/COMM ON to modify the USB power supply/communication settings.
❖ Select USB RAW CONV/BACKUP RESTORE to switch the connection mode.
❖ Use a USB cord to connect the camera to the computer. Next, switch the camera on.
❖ X RAW STUDIO should be launched.

Raw files can be edited with X RAW STUDIO.

Saving and Loading Settings with a Computer

❖ From the network/USB settings menu, select AUTO or POWER SUPPLY OFF/COMM ON to modify the USB power supply/communication settings.
❖ Select USB RAW CONV./BACKUP RESTORE to switch the connection mode.
❖ Use a USB connection to link the camera to a PC. Next, switch the camera on.
❖ Launch the Fujifilm TETHER application.

The FUJIFILM TETHER APP can be used to load or save camera settings.

Online Image Sharing

The X-M5 offers a number of helpful features for online ring photo sharing. With its integrated Frame.io Camera to Cloud technology, you can instantly begin uploading photos and videos as soon as you snap them by connecting wirelessly to a live internet connection. For photographers that need to collaborate with people remotely or share their work fast, this might be quite helpful. Additionally, the camera can pair with phones through Bluetooth, and when a picture is taken, it is instantly uploaded to the smartphone. The camera will continue to transfer pictures to the connected smartphone even when it is off if both Bluetooth and "Image Transfer While Power Off" are set on. Because there is no need for manual transfer, your photos are shared instantly, which can be particularly convenient for professionals who are constantly on the go. When sharing images online, keep in mind to abide by privacy and copyright rules. Always obtain consent before taking pictures of well-known individuals or private property, and be sure that no one's rights, or privacy are being violated by the images you post. Enjoy your shooting!

Methods for Sharing

To share your Fujifilm X-M5 photo online, take these actions:

❖ Download apps for your smartphone: You need to download at least one app before you can link your smartphone and camera. Install the app on your phone after downloading it from the Fujifilm website. Depending on the operating system on your phone, you may have different access to different applications.

❖ **Connect via Bluetooth:**
- Press the DISP/BACK button to view firing information.
- With "Bluetooth" highlighted, choose "OK" or "MENU."
- Click **MENU/OK** after selecting **PAIRING**. Connect your phone to the camera and open the app. The phone and camera will instantly pair via Bluetooth after the setup is finished. A white Bluetooth sign and a smartphone symbol will appear on the camera's screen once the connection has been made.

❖ **Posting Images:**
- Photographs taken with **ON** selected in Bluetooth/SMARTPHONE SETTING > AUTO IMAGE TRANSFER ORDER will be sent to the device that is associated with it.
- You may enable uploads to the linked device even while the camera is turned off by choosing **IMAGE TRANSFER WHILE POWER OFF** in the **CONNECTION SETTING** menu and **ON for Bluetooth/SMARTPHONE SETTING > Bluetooth ON/OFF**.
- Select "ON" under Bluetooth/SMARTPHONE SETTING > RESIZE IMAGE FOR SMARTPHONE to reduce photos for uploading to smartphones.

❖ **Choosing Images to Upload**
- Select **IMAGE TRANSFER ORDER** > select FRAMES from the **Playback Menu** to send pictures to a Bluetooth-enabled phone or tablet.
- Images can be transferred to a computer using PC AutoSave. Make sure you have the latest version of FUJIFILM PC AutoSave installed on your computer before sharing images from your camera via Wi-Fi.

When sharing images online, keep in mind to abide by privacy and copyright rules. Make sure no one's rights or privacy is violated by the photos you post.

CHAPTER SEVENTEEN
KNOWING COMPATIBILITY & LENSES

Fujifilm's native X-mount lenses

The Fujifilm X-Mount, a versatile and widely used lens mount designed for the company's mirrorless cameras, is included with the Fujifilm X-M5. A wide variety of lenses, such as prime lenses for crisp images and zoom lenses for more framing options, work incredibly well with the X-Mount. You can easily customize the camera to meet your unique needs by experimenting with the various settings, whether you're taking still photos or videos. The X-Mount lenses from Fujifilm are made with premium optics and craftsmanship to make sure you get the most out of your X-M5. When mounted on the X-M5, the focal lengths of these lenses will be 1.5 times their stated value because they are specifically designed for Fujifilm's APS-C sensor and have a 1.5x crop factor. **The following are the main categories into which the X-Mount lens portfolio is separated:**

❖ **Fixed focal length prime lenses:** For photographers who desire fast apertures and high-quality images, prime lenses are perfect. Their fixed focal lengths encourage creative composition, but they don't zoom. The prime lenses from Fujifilm are renowned for their exceptional bokeh, sharpness, and contrast, all of which enhance the overall appeal of your images.

- **Fujinon XF 23mm f/2 R WR:** This lightweight, weatherproof prime lens is live and has a 35mm equivalent focal length. It's perfect for street photography, portraiture, and general-purpose shooting because of its ring-fast autofocus and crisp image quality.

- **Fujinon XF 35mm f/1.4 R:** This lens is a classic 50mm equivalent that produces stunning bokeh and exceptional low-light performance. This lens produces a narrow depth of field and is perfect for portraits and low-light photography.

- **Fujinon XF 56mm f/1.2 R:** This portrait lens provides excellent bokeh and subject isolation. It's a great option for people who want to capture a dreamy, cinematic atmosphere or who take pictures of events or portraits.

❖ **Zoom lenses:** By enabling you to alter your framing without switching lenses, zoom lenses offer adaptability. For photographers and video artists who need a range of focal lengths in a single lens, zoom lenses are incredibly helpful.

- Often called the "kit lens," the Fujinon XF 18-55mm f/2.8-4 R LM OIS Lens is a flexible zoom lens with a wide-to-standard zoom range (27-82.5mm equivalent). With its optical image stabilization (OIS) ring, which is particularly helpful in low light or for filming video, this lens is excellent for daily photography.

- **Fujinon XF 16-80mm f/4 R OIS WR:** This lens is perfect for general-purpose, travel, and landscape photography because of its larger focal range (24-

120mm equivalent). It's a multipurpose workhorse lens with a steady f/4 aperture and weather resistance.

- **Fujinon XF 50-140mm f/2.8 R LM OIS WR:** This lens produces excellent images and is appropriate for portrait, sports, and wildlife photography. Because of its continuous f/2.8 aperture and OIS, it also does well in low light conditions.

❖ **Wide-angle lenses:** For astrophotography, landscape, and architectural photography, wide-angle lenses are perfect because they let you capture expansive scenes in fine detail.

- **Fujinon XF 14mm f/2.8 R:** Because of its sharpness and minimal distortion, the Fujinon XF 14mm f/2.8 R lens is perfect for landscape and architectural photography.
- The Fujinon XF 10-24mm f/4 R OIS WR lens, which has a wide zoom range and is 15-36mm equivalent, offers a versatile alternative. With picture stabilization, it's ideal for photographing wide landscapes or confined interior spaces.

❖ **Macro Lenses:** Because they enable precise capturing of minute details, macro lenses are perfect for close-up photography. High-quality macro lenses from Fujifilm are available for taking stunning pictures of small objects like flowers, insects, and textures.

- Using the Fujinon XF 80mm f/2.8 R LM OIS WR Macro, you can capture life-sized images of small subjects thanks to its 1:1 reproduction ratio. With built-in weather sealing and image stabilization, it's a great option for wildlife and product photographers.

❖ **Fisheye Lenses:** A "bubble" impression is created by the dramatic curvature of fisheye lenses, which offer an ultra-wide-angle vision. For imaginative and artistic photography, these lenses are perfect.

- **Fujinon XF 8mm f/3.5 R Fisheye:** This lens produces a unique fisheye perspective as it has an 8mm focal length (12mm equivalent). For people who like to experiment with perspective in their photos, it's perfect.

❖ **Telephoto Lenses:** Telephoto lenses are perfect for sports, wildlife, and long-distance views because they provide superior magnification and compression effects for both photos and videos.

- Fujinon XF 100-400mm f/4.5-5.6 R LM OIS WR: A robust telephoto zoom lens with a focal range of 150-600mm. Perfect for anyone who wants to clearly capture distant sights, including wildlife photographers.

❖ **Lens Compatibility:** The compatibility of the X-Mount on the Fujifilm X-M5 with both native Fujifilm lenses and a variety of third-party lenses is one of its most important characteristics. X-Mount lenses are produced by Sigma, Tamron, and Viltrox, expanding your options for certain requirements such as manual focus lenses, low-cost solutions, and uncommon focal lengths. For many customers, third-party lenses are still an affordable and practical option even though they might not offer as much integration as Fujifilm's original lenses (for instance, autofocus performance might be slower or smoother).

Selecting the Proper Lens for You

When selecting lenses for your Fujifilm X-M5, consider your preferences and shooting style. The XF 35mm f/1.4 R is a great example of a quick prime lens if you like taking street or portrait photos. For travel or daily use, a zoom lens (such as the XF 18-55mm f/2.8-4 R) is suitable if you need versatility. Lenses featuring image stabilization and smooth autofocus, like the XF 18-55mm, are perfect for videographers. With the Fujifilm X-M5's X-Mount system, you may select from a variety of lenses to fit almost any type of photography, including landscape, portrait, wildlife, and video.

The most suitable lenses for photography and videography

For your Fujifilm X-M5 to reach its full potential in both photography and filmmaking, choosing the appropriate lenses is essential. With a 26.1-megapixel APS-C sensor and compatibility with a wide variety of X-mount lenses, the X-M5 was released in late 2024. The best recommendations that fit various shooting tendencies are shown below.

Conventional Zoom Lenses

- ❖ **Fujinon XF 16-55mm f/2.8 R LM WR II:** Originally released with the X-M5, the Fujinon XF 16-55mm f/2.8 R LM WR II lens boasts a wide focal length range of 24-84mm in 35mm terminology. With a weight of about 0.90 lb, it is far lighter than its predecessor and may be used for a range of genres, such as portraits and landscapes. Performance is guaranteed to be constant in a range of lighting settings because to the fixed f/2.8 aperture.
- ❖ **Sigma 18-50mm f/2.8 DC DN Contemporary:** The focal length range of this third-party lens is 27-75mm. Although it sacrifices some breadth at the wide-angle end, its constant f/2.8 aperture and small, light design make it a good option for people who want mobility without sacrificing image quality.

Wide-angle lenses

- ❖ Sigma 10-18mm f/2.8 DC DN Contemporary: This lens is perfect for people who like to take wide-angle photos because it has an equivalent focal length of 15-27mm. It is ideal for architectural videography and landscape photography because to its compact size and continuous f/2.8 aperture.
- ❖ Fujinon XF 16mm f/1.4 R WR: This prime lens is a favorite among street and landscape photographers because to its narrow depth of field, clarity, and fast f/1.4 aperture. It also performs exceptionally well in low light conditions.

Portrait Lenses

- ❖ Fujinon XF 35mm f/1.4 R: Known for its clarity and beautiful bokeh, the Fujinon XF 35mm f/1.4 R prime lens, which is equal to 52.5mm, is perfect for portrait shooting in low light.
- ❖ Viltrox 23mm f/1.4: With its sharpness and 35mm equivalent focal length, the Viltrox 23mm f/1.4 lens is perfect for street photography and capturing unscripted moments.

Telephoto Lenses

- ❖ With an equivalent focal length of 75-210mm, the Fujinon XF 50-140mm f/2.8 R LM OIS WR lens offers a wide range that is ideal for wildlife, sports, and portrait photography. Clear photos are guaranteed across the zoom range thanks to the constant f/2.8 aperture and optical image stabilization.
- ❖ Fujinon XF 500mm f/5.6 OIS WR: This super-telephoto lens, which was unveiled in late 2024, is perfect for sports and wildlife photography. Long-distance photography is made easier by its optical image stabilization.

Macro Lenses

- ❖ With a 1:1 magnification ratio, the Fujinon XF 80mm f/2.8 R LM OIS WR Macro is a dedicated macro lens that is perfect for close-up shots. Its weather-resistant construction and optical image stabilization make it more versatile in a range of shooting conditions.

Focus length, aperture, size, weight, and specific shooting needs should all be taken into account when selecting a lens. Because the Fujifilm X-M5 works with so many different lenses, photographers and filmmakers can find the one that best suits their artistic vision.

The compatibility of third-party lenses

The Fujifilm X-M5's X-Mount lens system is compatible with a large selection of third-party lenses, providing photographers and videographer's greater options. Third-party lenses like Sigma, Tamron, Samyang, and Viltrox can provide a more specialized or cost-effective alternative, even though Fujifilm's original lenses are renowned for their superb performance and integration with their cameras. Regarding focal lengths, aperture sizes, and other characteristics, these lenses are highly adaptable.

Option for Third-Party Lenses

The following lists some of the leading third-party producers of lenses for the Fujifilm X-Mount along with what to expect from them:

- ❖ **Sigma:** In the market for third-party lenses for Fujifilm X-Mount cameras, Sigma has had a significant impact. When compared to Fujifilm's own lenses, theirs are renowned for their outstanding optical quality, robust construction, and affordable price.

- The Sigma 16mm f/1.4 DC DN Contemporary is a great substitute for anyone looking for a fast, large-aperture, wide-angle prime lens (24mm equivalent). Because of its sharpness and low-light capabilities, it is especially well-liked by street photographers, vloggers, and videographers.
- For everyday photography and portraits, the Sigma 30mm f/1.4 DC DN Contemporary lens (45mm equivalent) is a well-liked option. It performs exceptionally well in low light thanks to its large aperture, which also produces beautiful bokeh and shallow depth of field.
- **Sigma 56mm f/1.4 DC DN Contemporary:** With its superb subject isolation, silky bokeh, and fine details, this portrait lens (84mm equivalent) is perfect for portraiture. It is also compact and light.

❖ **The Tamron:** Tamron lenses are renowned for their affordability and adaptability. In addition to being reasonably priced, they produce lenses with excellent optics and functionality.
- **Tamron 11-20mm f/2.8 Di** is a wide-aperture, ultra-wide zoom lens (16-30mm equivalent) that is perfect for astrophotography and landscape photography. Its fast f/2.8 aperture is perfect for low light conditions and gives you more control over depth of field.
- **Tamron 17-70mm f/2.8 Di:** This adaptable zoom lens, which has a continuous f/2.8 aperture and covers a standard zoom range, is equivalent to 25-105mm. For anyone searching for a high-quality walk-around lens that is also fast enough for photography in low light, this is an excellent all-around lens.

❖ **Samyang:** Samyang (also known as Rokinon in some countries) is well-known for making ring lenses at lower prices than Fujifilm and other third-party makers. Although Samyang lenses are usually manual focus, they are well known for their excellent optical quality and affordability.
- A wide-angle prime lens (18mm equivalent) that works well for landscape and architecture photography is the Samyang 12mm f/2.0 NCS CS. It is especially well-liked for night sky photography because of its quick f/2.0 aperture, which makes it excellent in low light conditions.
- The large aperture of the Samyang 50mm f/1.2 AS UMC lens (75mm equivalent) allows for beautiful bokeh and efficient subject isolation. It is well-liked for artistic photography and portraits despite its manual focus.

❖ **Viltrox:** In the market for third-party lenses, Viltrox is a rising star. The company is renowned for creating low-cost autofocus lenses with excellent optical quality. A variety of prime and zoom lenses, many with fast aperture rings and sturdy construction, are available for the Fujifilm X-Mount.
- The Viltrox 23mm f/1.4 AF prime lens (35mm equivalent) offers flawless bokeh and exceptional low-light performance. Additionally, it has autofocus, which is a huge plus for anyone who would rather use autofocus than manual lenses.

- Because of its fast aperture and clear subject representation, the Viltrox 56mm f/1.4 AF lens (84mm equivalent) is perfect for portraiture. It is renowned for its high-quality images and features a good autofocus system.
- With its excellent subject isolation and bokeh, the Viltrox 85mm f/1.8 AF lens (127.5mm equivalent) is perfect for telephoto and portrait photography. For photo and video applications, it also features autofocus.

Third-Party Lens Considerations

Although using third-party lenses with the Fujifilm X-M5 is a great way to increase your options, there are a few things to keep in mind.

- ❖ **Autofocus Performance:** Although autofocus is a feature of many third-party lenses, it might not always be as fast or precise as native lenses from Fujifilm. Slower autofocus speed and accuracy are possible, especially when using lenses designed for other camera systems that have been modified for the Fujifilm X-Mount.
- ❖ **Firmware Upgrades for Lenses:** When new cameras are released, some third-party lenses can need firmware updates to ensure compatibility with the most recent camera models. To ensure optimum performance, be sure to check the lens manufacturer's website for firmware updates.
- ❖ **Autofocus vs. Manual Focus:** Certain third-party lenses, particularly those made by Samyang, only work with manual focus. For some types of photography (such landscapes and astrophotography), this can be a great solution, but it might not work well for things that move quickly or for videos that require autofocus.
- ❖ **Build and Image Quality:** Although a lot of third-party lenses perform well optically, you could find that they are not as robust as native lenses from Fujifilm. Features like weather sealing and lens coatings might be less advanced than those found in Fujifilm's high-end lenses, and the build quality varies.
- ❖ **Price vs. Performance:** For those on a tight budget, third-party lenses are a great option because they are often less expensive than Fujifilm's own lenses. They can produce high-quality images at a lower cost, but the overall design or focusing performance may suffer as a result.

Options for Adapters and Manual Focus

The Fujifilm X-M5 offers photographers and videographers a versatile platform, especially when using the ring focus function and several lens adapters. Your creative capacity can be significantly enhanced by being aware of these traits.

Adapters for lenses

A wide variety of lenses are compatible with the X-M5's X-mount system, and you can expand your lens selection using adapters.

- ❖ **Fujifilm M Mount Adapter:** This lens adapter allows the X-M5 to use M Mount lenses. High-quality materials are used in its three-part structure to ensure a precise fit and electrical connections that allow the lens and camera body to communicate flawlessly. The adapter has a function button that makes choosing lens settings easy.

❖ **Third-Party Adapters:** Leica M to Fujifilm X mount adapter is one of the adapters that Urth sells. These adapters are finely machined to offer a tight, light-sealed, and secure connection. They do not, however, provide automatic functions, therefore human focus and exposure setting adjustments are required.

It's important to keep in mind that depending on the lens and adapter combination, using adapters may result in limitations like vignetting, a loss of autofocus capabilities, or reduced image quality.

Options for Manual Focus

The X-M5 has a lot of features that help with manual focusing, guaranteeing accuracy and ease of use:

❖ **Manual Focus Indicator:** This on-screen indicator shows the depth of field as a blue bar and the distance to the subject inside the focus region as a white line. This visual aid makes it easier to decide which area of the scene will appear sharp.

❖ **Focus Check feature:** When manually adjusted, the camera's focus check feature magnifies the desired focus region, enabling precise fine-tuning. Reaching critical sharpness in complex issues requires this capacity.

❖ **Focus Peaking:** This feature makes it easier to spot the sharpest areas of the image by emphasizing in-focus areas with a colorful outline. The peaking color and intensity can be altered by users to suit their preferences and shooting conditions.

To activate and set up these manual focus aids, navigate to your X-M5's AF/MF SETTING menu and select the appropriate settings under MF ASSIST. Getting to know these tools will greatly enhance your manual focusing experience and provide you greater control over your compositions. You may be able to use a greater variety of lenses and accomplish precise focus in your photography and filmmaking endeavors by using adapters and mastering manual focus techniques.

CHAPTER EIGHTEEN
ABOUT ACCESSORIES AND EXPANSION

Suggested Memory Cards

Make sure the memory card you select for your Fujifilm X-M5 satisfies both the camera's specifications and your shooting needs. The X-M5 supports UHS-I for faster writing speeds and is capable of reading SD, SDHC, and SDXC memory cards. But not all memory cards are created equal, and choosing the finest one could have a significant impact on reliability, performance, and the shooting experience as a whole.

Performance and Speed Class

When choosing a memory card for the X-M5, write speed is the most crucial factor to take into account. The camera can take 6.2K video and take high-resolution pictures, so you'll need a card that can handle these data-intensive tasks. Continuous shooting, burst photography, and 4K/6K video recording are best suited for cards with higher write speeds, including UHS-I U3 or V30. Higher write speeds and bigger file sizes can be handled by these cards without resulting in buffer issues or missing frames. Higher write speeds will help the X-M5, especially when shooting RAW or capturing high-quality video. When taking burst sequences of high-resolution photos or recording 4K video, a UHS-I U3 card with a minimum write speed of 30MB/s will operate flawlessly.

Capacity for Storage

Next, check the amount of storage on the memory card. SD cards with capacities ranging from a few megabytes to 1TB are compatible with the X-M5, which should be sufficient for the majority of photographers and videographers. A 64GB or 128GB card is a good place to start if you're shooting both 6.2K video and high-resolution stills. This eliminates the need for frequent card replacements and enables longer sessions. Those who frequently record video, especially at higher bit rates or at 6.2K quality, might find that a 256GB or 512GB card is a better choice. This removes the concern of running out of space during important sessions and allows for longer recording times and greater comfort.

Sturdiness and Dependability

Another important factor to take into account when choosing a memory card for the X-M5 is durability, particularly if you plan to shoot in difficult conditions. Choose cards that are resistant to shocks, water, and extreme temperatures. Even though the X-M5 is lightweight, if you're out in inclement weather, like rain or snow, its compact size may make it susceptible to the elements. Therefore, using a card that is made to withstand these situations is the best option. These days, a lot of cards include integrated dust, water, and impact resistance, guaranteeing that your data is safe even under less-than-ideal conditions. For instance, cards with high durability ratings, such as SanDisk and Lexar, are made to resist physical damage without compromising the integrity of the ring data.

The Best Memory Card Options

❖ **SanDisk Extreme PRO SDXC UHS-I U3 V30:** This is a high-end option for people seeking reliability and speed. The SanDisk Extreme PRO is perfect for 4K video recording and quick burst shooting because it can read and write data at up to 170 MB/s and 90 MB/s, respectively. It is excellent for photography and cinematography and comes in a range of capacities. The card is incredibly durable and designed to withstand shock, water, and temperature changes.

❖ **Lexar Professional 1000x SDXC UHS-II U3:** The Lexar 1000x series offers UHS-II rates for blazingly quick performance. Even though the X-M5 does not fully utilize UHS-II rates, users can still benefit from the faster read and write speeds when moving data to a computer. With read rates of up to 150 MB/s and write speeds of up to 90 MB/s, the card is a great option for anyone who records high-quality video or shoots in continuous bursts.

❖ **Samsung EVO Plus 128GB SDXC UHS-I U3:** The Samsung EVO Plus is a more reasonably priced option that effectively balances price and performance. Photographers and videographers who want reliability but don't need high performance will love this card's read and write speeds of up to 100MB/s and 90MB/s, respectively. Additionally, the card is designed to withstand extremes of temperature, wetness, and magnetic fields, ensuring that it functions effectively under challenging conditions.

❖ For photographers and videographers, the Kingston Canvas React Plus 128GB SDXC UHS-I U3 is an additional great choice. It is perfect for 4K video recording and rapid continuous shooting because it can read and write data at up to 100 MB/s and 80 MB/s, respectively. It is also designed to resist X-rays, stress, and water. ring.

Gimbals and tripods for stability

With the Fujifilm X-M5, using the right tripod or gimbal can greatly improve the steadiness and quality of your photos and videos. You don't need the most expensive or powerful stabilizers because the X-M5 is a lightweight mirrorless camera, but you should still spend money on gear that provides steady support and seamless operation.

Excellent Tripods for the X-M5 Fujifilm

A good tripod should be easy to adjust, lightweight, and long-lasting. **Whether you're taking long-exposure, landscape, or portrait photos, a sturdy tripod will help minimize unwanted camera shake.**

- ❖ **Excellent Tripods for the X-M5 Fujifilm:** For owners of a Fujifilm X-M5 who are looking for a tripod that is both lightweight and sturdy, the Manfrotto Befree Advanced is an excellent option. It is lightweight and strong enough to support mirrorless cameras because it is made of aluminum. It features a quick-release plate for easy installation and a ball head for smooth adjustments. Multiple locking angles on the legs make it simple to put up on uneven surfaces. This tripod's exceptional stability and ability to fold down to a tiny size make it perfect for travel photography.

- ❖ **Travel Tripods by Peak Design:** Designed specifically for photographers looking for a compromise between stability and mobility, this is one of the most unusual tripods on the market. The Peak Design Travel Tripod is convenient to carry in a bag because it folds up into a comparatively small container. With a weight capacity of up to 20 pounds, it offers remarkable strength and stability despite its small size. Additionally, it has a built-in phone mount, which is perfect for taking pictures on the go and making content for social media. Although the aluminum version is less expensive, the carbon fiber version is lighter.

- ❖ **Gitzo GT1545T, Traveler Series 1:** A great substitute for professional photographers looking for high-quality images is the Gitzo GT1545T. Because carbon fiber is used in its construction, it is both lightweight and incredibly durable. When taking timelapses or long-exposure photographs, this tripod's robustness and vibration resistance are crucial. Although the Fujifilm X-M5 is more costly than similar options, committed photographers will find that its accuracy and reliability make the cost worthwhile.

- ❖ **GorillaPod 3K by Joby:** The Joby GorillaPod 3K is a great option for vloggers and video producers that desire versatility. The legs of this tripod, in contrast to others, are pliable and can be wrapped around tree branches, railings, or poles. It lets you set up your camera in places where a conventional tripod wouldn't fit and experiment with different angles. It is a great lightweight option for handheld shooting and quick setups, but it is not suitable for long exposures or very stable images.

- ❖ **Benro Mach 3 Tripod with Carbon Fiber:** For those seeking a dependable all-purpose tripod that can manage a range of circumstances, the Benro Mach3 is a great option. It provides easy adjustments, superior build quality, and a large weight capacity. For photographers who travel regularly, the carbon fiber construction guarantees durability without adding extra weight. Additionally, it has adjustable feet that allow you to choose between spiked and rubber for better traction on different types of terrain.

Top Gimbals for the X-M5 Fujifilm

For filmmakers who want their films to have fluid, dramatic motion, a gimbal is essential. The X-M5 works with most small mirrorless camera gimbals because it is quite light. **Think about weight capacity, battery life, ease of setup, and sophisticated features like tracking and timelapse modes when choosing a gimbal.**

- ❖ **The DJI RS3 Mini:** One of the best gimbals for the Fujifilm X-M5 is the DJI RS 3 Mini. It is a great fit for the X-M5 because it is specifically designed for lightweight mirrorless cameras. The gimbal is lightweight and compact, yet it offers strong stabilization for the ring. It features a 1.4-inch touchscreen, a 10-hour battery life, and Bluetooth shutter control. Long shooting sessions are possible without fatigue because to the lightweight design.
- ❖ **Weebill Zhiyun 3:** Another great option for X-M5 users looking for a robust and reliable gimbal is the Zhiyun Weebill 3. Even with hefty lenses, its strong motor guarantees perfect stabilization. Its extensible sling grip and integrated wrist rest are two of its most noteworthy characteristics; they improve comfort during extended shooting sessions. Additionally, it has a built-in microphone and fill light, which makes it perfect for vloggers and independent video producers.
- ❖ **Moza Aircross 3:** Because it can be utilized in a number of shooting modes, such as handheld, briefcase, and dual-handle configurations, this gimbal is well-liked for its adaptability. Its strong motor allows mirrorless cameras like the Fujifilm X-M5 to stabilize smoothly. Additionally, the AirCross 3 has vertical shooting, which is perfect for content for social media. You can record continuously for longer because to its long battery life.
- ❖ **FeiyuTech Scorp.-C:** Despite being inexpensive, the FeiyuTech Scorp-C gimbal provides excellent stabilization for the Fujifilm X-M5. It is perfect for beginners because of its lightweight design and easy control system. Despite its low cost, it offers comfortable grip and fluid motion control, making it a great tool for general filmmaking and travel videography.
- ❖ **The DJI RS 3:** The full-size DJI RS 3 is a great option for seasoned filmmakers seeking a more advanced gimbal. It can handle larger lenses and accessories since its motors are stronger than those of the Mini version. Additionally, it features an enhanced stabilization algorithm for smoother film, a touchscreen for easy adjustments, and a clever auto-lock mechanism. Even though it is a little heavier and larger than the RS 3 Mini, it performs exceptionally well in demanding video applications.

External Audio Solutions and Microphones

The built-in microphones on the Fujifilm X-M5 are sufficient for simple recordings, but they might not have the clarity and detail needed for high-quality work when it comes to recording audio for your films. It is strongly advised to use an external microphone to enhance your audio, especially for vlogging, interviews, or dramatic movies. Because the

X-M5 features a microphone input, it may be used with a wide variety of external audio solutions that could greatly enhance the video's sound quality.

Comprehending the Audio Input of the Camera

You can connect extra microphones straight to the Fujifilm X-M5 thanks to its 3.5mm microphone connector. Although many microphones share this connection, you should make sure the microphone you choose is compatible with the X-M5 and has the required connections. More versatility during productions may be possible using the adapters that many microphones come with, and some even have wireless options.

External Microphone Types

Depending on your recording needs, you can choose from a wide variety of microphones. The main types that work well with the X-M5 are as follows.

- ❖ **Shotgun Microphones:** Because shotgun microphones are directional, they reduce background noise while gathering sound from a designated area. These microphones are ideal for focused recordings, such as interviews or lone commentary, and they come in particularly useful outside or in noisy settings. When you want to record sound from a particular subject without the surrounding environment interfering, they're also perfect for filmmaking.
  - **Rode VideoMic Pro+:** Because of its rechargeable battery, adjustable gain, and excellent sound quality, the Rode VideoMic Pro+ shotgun microphone is a well-liked option for filmmakers and video producers. The Rode VideoMic Pro+ is perfect for vlogs, interviews, and general video recording because of its supercardioid polar pattern, which isolates the speaker's voice.
  - **Sennheiser MKE 600:** During live performances, this premium shotgun microphone generates clear, concentrated sound. Its supercardioid shape reduces off-axis noise and efficiently reroutes sounds away from the subject. This microphone is perfect for filming outdoors or while on the go because it is also incredibly durable.
- ❖ **Lavalier Clip-On Microphones:** Often referred to as lapel mics, lavalier microphones are small, clip-on microphones that may be fastened to your clothing, typically around the chest or collar. They provide a hands-free option, which makes them perfect for presentations, interviews, and other situations where the subject is moving around. Lavalier microphones are perfect for situations involving a lot of speech since they capture audio from the speaker without requiring them to carry a microphone.
  - **Rode SmartLav+:** This inexpensive, high-quality lavalier microphone works well with the X-M5. The omnidirectional design ensures high-quality audio recording even when the subject moves or speaks at varied distances from the microphone. It connects via a 3.5mm connector.
  - **Sony ECM77B:** Perfect for formal interviews or documentaries, the Sony ECM77B is a high-end lapel microphone with superb audio quality. Because

of its broad frequency response, the microphone can clearly record a variety of sounds.

- ❖ **Systems of Wireless Microphones:** Additional mobility is made possible with wireless microphones, which is particularly helpful in situations involving movement, interviews, or situations when the speaker is far from the camera. These systems typically consist of a receiver (attached to the camera) and a transmitter (worn by the speaker). For outdoor photography, event coverage, and any other circumstance where wires could be an inconvenience, wireless solutions are perfect.
  - ▪ **Rode Wireless GO II:** This portable wireless microphone system offers convenient wireless connectivity and excellent audio quality. With built-in microphones on both the transmitter and receiver, it's easy to set up, but for more covert use, you can also add a lavalier mic. The gadget is excellent for vlogging, interviews, and mobile filmmaking because of its remarkable endurance and range.
  - ▪ **Sennheiser XSW-D Portable Lavalier Set:** This cordless wireless system records high-quality audio. This system is appropriate for brief deployments needing a reliable and portable wireless solution, and it comes with a lavalier microphone.
- ❖ **Stereo Microphones:** Stereo mics provide depth and richness to recordings and are perfect for capturing more natural-sounding audio. These are excellent for recording musical performances, background noise, or any situation where a more realistic sound experience is needed. They can also be used to give your surroundings a more balanced sound in vlogs while maintaining the speaker's main focus.
  - ▪ **Audio-Technica AT8024:** This versatile stereo shotgun microphone minimizes background noise while capturing high-quality sound. It works well for general-purpose video recording if you wish to record background noise without sacrificing the speaker's speech quality.
  - ▪ **Rode Stereo VideoMic X:** This device offers excellent stereo recording and is ideal for recording background noise in addition to voice. It is perfect for nature documentaries, music videos, and outdoor recordings since it incorporates a shock-mount mechanism to reduce handling noise and a high-pass filter to remove low-frequency noise.

Video Recording Audio Solutions

Controlling the processing and alteration of audio is another essential part of your X-M5 audio setup, in addition to microphones. **Some options to think about are:**

- ❖ **External Recorders of Audio:** Although external microphones can be used with the X-M5's built-in audio input, using a dedicated external audio recorder can enhance the quality of your sound, particularly under challenging recording circumstances. High-quality recordings are ensured by these recorders' superior preamps and more control over audio levels.

- **Zoom H5 Handy Recorder:** This compact audio recorder has multiple microphone inputs and produces high-quality sound. Because the microphone capsules are interchangeable, you can choose between shotgun and stereo configurations according to your needs.
- **Tascam DR-40X:** This well-liked portable recorder has various inputs for external microphones and built-in microphones for high-quality 4-track recording. It's a great option for recording high-quality audio and offering straightforward file management for quick transfers.

❖ **Interfaces for Audio:** An audio interface may connect your camera to XLR microphones, which are frequently used in professional settings, if you plan to record sound in a controlled situation (like a studio). This option may be useful for applications that require ring studio-quality sound, but it is more common for studio recording.
  - The Scarlett 2i2 is a well-liked USB audio interface that offers ring-perfect sound and preamps ideal for professional XLR microphones.

CHAPTER NINETEEN
DEBUGGING

This chapter delved into fixing issue you may be encountering while utilizing your camera. Please get in touch with your local Fujifilm distributor if you are unable to find the answer here.

Regarding power and battery

- ❖ **Issue:** The camera doesn't switch on.
- ❖ **Fix:**
  - ▪ When the battery is shipped, it is not charged. Prior to initial use, charge the battery.
  - ▪ Put in a completely charged spare battery or charge the current one.
  - ▪ Put back in the proper orientation.
  - ▪ Lock the cover of the battery chamber.
- ❖ **Issue:** The battery drains rapidly
- ❖ **Fix:**
  - ▪ Install the battery right before shooting and keep it warm in your pocket or another location while utilizing it in a low-temperature setting.
  - ▪ 🔲 [AF/MF SETTING] > [PRE-AF] should be set to [OFF].
  - ▪ Use 🔲 [SCREEN SET-UP] > [LCD BRIGHTNESS] to change the display's brightness.
  - ▪ Modify the 🔲 [POWER MANAGEMENT] configuration.
- ❖ **Issue:** Abruptly, the camera goes off.
- ❖ **Fix:**
  - ▪ Verify whether the battery is depleting.
  - ▪ The camera will automatically switch off when the time specified in 🔲 [POWER MANAGEMENT] > [AUTO POWER OFF] has passed.
  - ▪ The camera will automatically switch off when the temperature rises.
  - ▪ When using interval-timer photography, the screen will go blank if the shooting interval is too lengthy. When the shutter-release button is hit or a few seconds before shooting, the screen will return to normal.
- ❖ **Issue:** The camera doesn't shut down.
- ❖ **Fix:** Examine the indicator lamp.

Problems regarding charging

- ❖ **Issue:** The USB does not begin charging.
- ❖ **Fix:**

- The camera won't begin charging when it is switched on. Disconnect the power.
- By the time the battery is fully charged, charging will not begin.
- Verify that the camera, USB cords, and computer are all connected.
- Make sure the computer is turned on before charging from it.
- For safety, the charging process will not begin when the battery temperature is too high or too low. Before charging the battery once more, wait for its temperature to return to normal.

❖ **Issue:** It charges slowly.
❖ **Fix:** Charging may be sluggish for safety reasons when the battery temperature is too high or too low. Before charging the battery once more, wait for its temperature to return to normal.
❖ **Issue:** The battery doesn't charge even though the indicator lamp blinks.
❖ **Fix:** Use a soft dry cloth to clean the terminals.

The power supply problems

❖ **Issue:** The icon for the power supply is not visible.
❖ **Fix:** Verify that [USB POWER SUPPLY/COMM SETTING] has [POWER SUPPLY ON/COMM OFF] chosen.

Displays and menus problems

❖ **Issue:** The display language is not English.
❖ **Fix:** For 🔧 [USER SETTING], choose [ENGLISH] > 🌐 言語/LANG.

The shooting issues

The fundamental photography

❖ **Issue:** Pressing the shutter button does not take a picture.
❖ **Fix:**
- Verify that the storage medium is configured properly.
- Verify that the memory card's write-protect switch is not in the locked position.
- Examine the storage media's available space.
- When shooting without a memory card, choose [ON] for 🔧 [BUTTON/DIAL SETTING] > [SHOOT WITHOUT CARD].
- You might not be able to take pictures if [FOCUS] is chosen for 📷 [AF/MF SETTING] > [RELEASE/FOCUS PRIORITY].
- By choosing [ON] for 🔧 [BUTTON/DIAL SETTING] > [SHOOT WITHOUT LENS], you might be able to capture images if you're using a lens manufactured by someone else.

The video recording

- ❖ **Issue:** The video recording abruptly stopped.
- ❖ **Fix:** If the storage media's writing speed is slow, recording can halt. The Fujifilm website lists the storage media that are supported.

About Continuous Shooting (Burst Mode)

- ❖ **Issue:** The speed of the burst fire is reduced.
- ❖ **Fix:** A number of factors, including lens type, storage medium writing speed, flash use, exposure circumstances, camera settings, battery level, and ambient temperature, can cause the burst shooting speed to be slower.

The panorama

- ❖ **Issue:** Pressing the shutter button does not record a panorama.
- ❖ **Fix:** Wait for the indicator lights to go out.

Issue about face detection

- ❖ **Issue:** There is no face found.
- ❖ **Fix**
  - Clear the obstacles.
  - Make the subject's face take up more space in the frame by altering the composition.
  - Request that the person be facing the camera.
  - For 🔲 [AF/MF SETTING] > 👤 [FACE/EYE DETECTION SETTING], choose [FACE DETECTION ON].
  - Make sure the camera is level.
  - Shoot in a more favorable light.

The subject detection

- ❖ **Issue:** There is no subject found.
- ❖ **Fix:**
  - Select a position that will allow you to observe as much of the subject as possible.
  - To have your topic take up more of the frame, get closer to it.
  - For 🔲 [AF/MF SETTING] > [SUBJECT DETECTION SETTING], choose [SUBJECT DETECTION ON].
  - Use a better light for shooting.

Flash issue

❖ **Issue:** The flash doesn't activate.
❖ **Fix:**

- Verify the drive modes, ▣ [FLASH SETTING] > [FLASH FUNCTION SETTING], and ⚡ [SHOOTING SETTING] > [SHUTTER TYPE].
- Use an external flash only after reading the instructions.

❖ **Issue:** The subject is not fully illuminated by the flash
❖ **Fix:**
- Place the subject within the flash's range.
- Hold the camera properly.
- Even when the flash fires, the image may appear darker if the shutter speed is greater than the sync speed. Select a shutter speed that is either slower than or equal to the sync speed.

Photographic abnormalities

❖ **Issue:** The image appears hazy and out of focus.
❖ **Fix:**
- Choose a different focus mode than manual focus.
- When capturing photos, use a tripod. Using the self-timer shooting feature and the remote release is also advised.
- To prevent camera shake when shooting handheld, keep the camera steady and lightly touch the shutter-release button.
- Activate the picture stabilization feature on the camera.
- Turn on the image stabilization feature while using a lens that has it.
- In dimly lit areas, the shutter speed could be slower. Employ a flash, raise the ISO sensitivity, or use a quicker shutter speed.
- Lock focus and exposure when you shoot.
- The attention area should be expanded by a few steps.

❖ **Issue:** Either the subject is distorted, or the camera captures pictures of nonexistent objects.
❖ **Fix:** Because of light reflection and other factors, pictures may capture some occurrences that are invisible to the human sight.
❖ **Issue:** Images are streaked.
❖ **Fix:** This is not a sign of a fault; it is normal.
- Choose [PIXEL MAPPING] > H[IMAGE QUALITY SETTING].
- Bright patches of different hues, including white, red, and blue, can be caused by X-rays, cosmic rays, and other radiation types interacting with the image sensor. Such bright patches are less common because to pixel mapping.

❖ **Issue:** The photo captures noise.
❖ **Fix:** Before using, turn off the power for a moment.

Playback problems

The full-frame playback

- ❖ **Issue:** The images are hazy.
- ❖ **Fix:** The images were captured using a camera of a different brand or model.
- ❖ **Issue:** Zoom playback is not available.
- ❖ **Fix:** The images were taken with a different brand or type of camera or with [RESIZE].

Video playback issue

- ❖ **Issue:** The movie is playing without sound.
- ❖ **Fix:**
  - Change the volume of the playback
  - When filming a movie, avoid blocking the microphone.
  - Avoid obstructing the speaker while it is playing.

Deletion issue

- ❖ **Issue:** After selecting [ERASE] > [ALL FRAMES], the selected images are kept and not erased.
- ❖ **Fix:** A portion of the images chosen for removal are protected. Remove the protection using the same tool that was used to apply it initially.

Frame number issue

- ❖ **Issue:** Suddenly, the file numbering is reset.
- ❖ **Fix:** The camera was turned on and the battery-chamber cover was opened. Before opening the battery-chamber lid, turn off the camera.

Problems occurring during connection

Issue about TV connection

- ❖ **Issue:** The screen is blank.
- ❖ **Fix:** In playback mode, the camera screen will not show anything when it is linked to a television.
- ❖ **Issue:** There is no sound or image on the TV.
- ❖ **Fix:**
  - Make sure the camera is connected correctly.
  - Select "HDMI" as the input.
  - To change the volume, use the television's controls.
  - Verify the TV side's supported resolution and frame rate.

Connection to computers problem

- ❖ **Issue:** The camera is not recognized by the computer.
- ❖ **Fix:**
  - Verify the USB cable and make sure it is properly reconnected.
  - Before attaching the camera, make sure the connection mode is set for the purpose for which it will be used.
  - Configure the camera connection mode to work with the computer's program. Additionally, examine the computer's application's settings.

Connection to smartphones problem

- ❖ **Issue:** Unable to connect to iPads or iPhones.
- ❖ **Fix:** For [USB POWER SUPPLY/COMM SETTING], [POWER SUPPLY ON/COMM OFF] is chosen. When the camera is connected to a device that does not supply power via a Lightning connection, choose [POWER SUPPLY OFF/COMM ON].
- ❖ **Issue:** Unable to access a smartphone for a connection
- ❖ **Fix:** Depending on the kind of connector that the smartphone has, there are several steps involved in connecting the camera.

About Wireless transfer issue

- ❖ **Issues:**
  - Cannot establish a connection with a smartphone.
  - The smartphone's camera takes a long time to connect or upload images.
  - The upload is interrupted or fails.
- ❖ **Fix:**
  - Bring the gadgets closer together.
  - Keep the camera away from radio-emitting gadgets.
- ❖ **Issue:** The photos cannot be uploaded.
- ❖ **Fix:**
  - Only one device at a time can be connected to the smartphone and camera. Cut off the connection and try again.
  - Make another attempt to connect. It may be challenging to connect when there are several devices around.
  - Images taken with other devices might not be able to be uploaded to the camera.
  - It takes a while to upload movies. Additionally, videos in formats that cellphones do not allow may not be able to be uploaded.

Additional issues

Operation of the Camera

- ❖ **Issue:** The camera is not responding.
- ❖ **Fix:**
  - Take out the battery and put it back in.
  - Put in a completely charged spare battery or charge the current one.
  - Verify the mode of the LAN or USB connection.
  - To unlock the controls, press and hold the [MENU/OK] button.
  - Verify the indication lamp's illumination condition. Replace the battery and see whether the camera still works if the issue continues.
  - To see if the buttons are locked, select 🄵 [BUTTON/DIAL SETTING] > [LOCK].
- ❖ **Issue:** The camera isn't working properly.
- ❖ **Fix:** Take out the battery and put it back in. If the issue continues, get in touch with your Fujifilm dealer.

Sound issue

- ❖ **Issue:** There was no sound.
- ❖ **Fix:** Modify the volume

"Q" (The Quick Menu) issue

- ❖ **Issue:** The quick menu is not displayed when the [Q] button is pressed.
- ❖ **Fix:** Terminate TTL-LOCK.

FINAL SUMMARY

Regardless of experience level, the Fujifilm X-M5 is a great camera for anyone looking to take or produce high-quality photos and videos. It is lightweight, easy to use, and loaded with practical features including fast focusing and a sharp 26.1MP sensor. Whether you're shooting smooth 6.2K video or making an incredible photo ring, this camera is designed to provide professional results. Choose the right accessories for your X-M5 to get the most out of it. Memory cards, microphones, and lenses all contribute to making the entire experience better. You can select the lens that best suits your style because the camera is compatible with a variety of lenses. Choosing a fast memory card can help you save your photos and videos faster. Purchasing an external microphone to enhance sound quality can also give your movies a polished appearance. You can easily capture exceptional content with the Fujifilm X-M5 if you set it up properly, whether you're shooting photos, videos, or both!